Starting School   *A study in policies*

Starting School
A study in policies

Richard Palmer

 University of London Press Ltd

372.1
PAL

0036513

ISBN 0 340 08000 0 ✓

University of London Press Ltd
St Paul's House, Warwick Lane, London EC4P 4AH
Printed and bound in Great Britain by
Hazell Watson & Viney Ltd, Aylesbury, Bucks

64124

Leeds.

Contents

List of flow diagrams

To the memory of Dr A. G. Hughes
Chief Inspector, London County Council 1947-56

Foreword

When I was first appointed Chairman of the Central Advisory Council for Education (England), which finally produced *Children and their Primary Schools,* I visited various primary schools in and around London. One of the outstanding infant headmistresses in London, at the first school I visited, urged that something should be done for the 'summer children'. I must confess that at that moment I did not fully understand their problems. But it was with real pride and pleasure that I telephoned to this headmistress on the morning of the publication of the Report to tell her that we had indeed 'done something' about them. With our recommendations for an expansion of nursery provision, more flexibility in entry, part-time entry, and a longer infant stage of schooling, the summer children would have benefited.

But alas, recommendations are not necessarily followed by action, and our recommendations for a large expansion of nursery provision, and changes in methods and ages of entry (this last requiring legislation) have not yet been implemented, although I think it can truthfully be said that they have coloured thinking on these matters.

Richard Palmer, writing from long experience as leader of the primary team of the ILEA Inspectorate, looks again in the pages that follow, and in great detail, at our proposals for nursery provision and entry to school. He has produced a modification of the plan we suggested, which has been called the *London Plan* (although it should more accurately be described as the 'Palmer Plan'). He has calculated the cost, both in money and in personnel. This is more than a theoretical cost, as it has been worked out in relation to schools in two London districts, Peckham and Brixton. It is a mammoth and most valuable exercise which he has completed.

I find now his *London Plan* an improvement on our *Interim Plan,* which itself I personally came to prefer to our *Long-term Plan.* There are points on which my emphasis might differ from his, but these are points of detail rather than of principle. For instance, I am perhaps more confident than he that *voluntary* half-time attendance of summer-born

9

rising-fives would suffice to ensure that all children who need to attend that term would do so. In this case, to introduce compulsion in order to protect the very small minority of children with inadequate parents seems to be taking a sledge hammer to crack a nut. Rather should the emphasis be on more help for the inadequate family.

On a point of slightly more substance, I would emphasise, perhaps even more than he has done, the continuation of playgroups, first, because in the short-run it will be necessary, and second, because of the part that they play in parental education and parental involvement. Like him, I would hope that, with a greater emphasis on improving their quality, they might continue to make a useful contribution in association with the maintained system.

Both the 'Plowden' plans and the *London Plan* require a large expansion in the number of nursery assistants. It cannot be said too strongly that the training of these assistants should not be considered purely as an expense attributable to schools; indeed, in London, it already comes out of the Further Education budget. It *is* a form of further education for prospective mothers, with general education included, as well as a means of training staff for nurseries. We do not hesitate to train engineers, plumbers or hairdressers. It is equally important to train mothers, for on their quality depends the future of their children.

As well as describing this new possible form of organisation, Richard Palmer has written sensitively and wisely about the problems of the young child on entry to school and of his development thereafter, and stresses the importance of continuity and overlap between the nursery and infant stages. This is valuable; much in our present system is excellent, but there is still room for more flexibility of approach and for a new look at what actually happens.

A change in organisation by itself cannot alter attitudes, but it can make new thinking easier. We need urgently to try a new pattern of entry to school. I can only endorse Richard Palmer's eloquent and well-argued plea for permissive legislation to make it possible to put into practice experiments such as his *London Plan*. It may not be the final solution; modifications may be necessary, particularly for regions with different circumstances. The first step is legislation to allow a changed pattern.

BRIDGET PLOWDEN

Introduction

The great importance of education in early childhood has long been recognised, though little until recently has been done to expand nursery education. It remained for the Plowden Council to realise that such an expansion needs to be linked with a review of the whole pattern for starting school, so that the vital transition from home to school will be gradual and geared to the needs of each child.

But the Plowden proposals, though a very great advance, are not necessarily the last word. In 1969, with the great encouragement of Lady Plowden herself, I undertook in consultation with colleagues a review for the ILEA of various 'Plowden-type' proposals for starting school. The outcome was a further scheme which came to be known as the 'London Plan'. Tested against the actual circumstances of forty London schools, it proved to be very economical of scarce resources, and therefore to give hope of the speedy achievement of nursery education as 'thick on the ground' as infant education. Still more important (as Lady Plowden points out in her foreword), it seemed to go even further than Plowden in achieving a right pattern for starting school, and in viewing the education of early childhood as a continuous whole.

This book leads up to a detailed account of the *London Plan* itself, but this is seen in a much wider context presented in the earlier chapters. Thus we begin with an account of the general structure of primary education in England and Wales, with its curious anomaly, the 'birthday handicap', which can lead to inequality of opportunity at the very outset of schooling. We go on to consider some of the ways in which the transition from home to infant school can be made easier and more gradual, even under present arrangements. We then look at what provision is now made for young children before they reach the infant stage, and at the modern case for expanding nursery education. So the ground is prepared for examining the various proposals made to Plowden, and by Plowden, for achieving a better pattern, and twelve criteria are set out by which we can know it when we find it. So we come to the *London Plan* itself, which is tested in detail against our twelve criteria, and its cost examined. Finally, we look beyond these matters of policy to the wider perspectives in the education of early childhood which a fresh pattern for starting school could reveal.

To have tried to describe the slightly different Scottish arrangements in the same context as those south of the border would have added greatly to my difficulties and the reader's, and no disrespect is intended to a country with great educational traditions. But the needs of children are much the same everywhere, and I hope that this discussion of their problems in starting school will also be of value to Scottish readers and that perhaps some form of the *London Plan* may find favour there.

Many have contributed both to the *London Plan* itself and to the making of this book. Several former colleagues in the ILEA had a notable share in both. I think particularly of Miss Nora Goddard, who was a close collaborator in my work on the *London Plan* and also read the whole book in draft. Her ideas have influenced me greatly throughout our many years of work together; in this book, they are especially evident in chapter 2. Other former colleagues have also given me great help and encouragement, especially Dr E. W. H. Briault, Dr Leonard Payling, Miss Gwen Clemens, Mrs Ivy Owen, and Miss Audrey Babb. My daughter and son-in-law, Drs Elizabeth and John Newson, not only had some share in the earlier discussions, but read the typescript; their expert advice on the social psychology of early childhood has been invaluable. My daughter Gillian Newson brought skill and patience to the execution of the flow-diagrams. My wife, Mary Palmer, as always, was my most valued critic in matters of style and clarity, reading the whole book in untidy first draft, and tolerating cheerfully a first year of retirement to the sound of a typewriter. Finally, I must express my deep gratitude to Lady Plowden, who not only wrote me a generous foreword, but read the typescript with the care and understanding and sense of values that are so characteristic of her. Her encouragement throughout has been an inspiration. I ought to add that neither she nor others who have read the book in draft should be held committed to every opinion it contains.

My former chief, Dr A. G. Hughes, knew that I was writing this book and I had looked forward to presenting it to him for his blessing. To the grief of many, he died last year. He contributed to educational thinking in the London Education Service perhaps as much as any man since Thomas Henry Huxley. I am proud to dedicate this book to his memory.

Black Bourton, Oxford   RICHARD PALMER
January 1971

CHAPTER I | # The Structure of Primary Education

AGES AND STAGES

This book is about beginning school: what is wrong with our present pattern and how we can get it right. But to see this problem in perspective, we must first look at the general structure of primary education as a whole, at what Plowden* called its 'ages and stages'. The 'ages' are not altogether simple, for reasons which will appear presently. The 'stages' are three: the nursery stage, which is voluntary, and the infant and junior stages, which are compulsory. This chapter, then, will deal with the broad pattern of primary education, but especially with the infant and junior stages, and the way children flow through them, from home to infant school, from infants to juniors, and from juniors to secondary schools.

This would be easy to describe if, by some combination of biological and administrative ingenuity, it could be ensured that all children were born on the same educationally convenient date —for example, 1 September. Ages and stages would then correspond precisely. Children would enter school at just five, go on to the juniors at just seven, and transfer to secondary school at just eleven. No doubt there would be complaints from overloaded maternity hospitals—and from the children themselves about the lack of any joyful scatter of birthday parties. And it is a moot point, as we shall see later, whether a machine-like precision in the age of entry to school is educationally desirable. However,

---

* *Children and their Primary Schools* (HMSO 1967), chapter 10. This Report (in two volumes) of the Central Advisory Council for Education (England), under the Chairmanship of Lady Plowden, is commonly known as the Plowden Report. I shall make constant reference to it in this book and for brevity will follow the common practice of referring to it simply as 'Plowden'. In most cases reference will be to the numbered paragraphs of volume I.

13

in describing the structure of primary education it would simplify matters considerably.

Instead, children's birthdays scatter almost (though not quite) evenly throughout the year. Indeed, it is the problem of reconciling this happy and natural situation with administrative feasibility, on the one hand, and the needs of individual children, on the other, that this book is largely about. But it does make the flow of children through primary education, the relation between ages and stages, quite hard to describe. In understanding such a description, not everyone is helped by flow diagrams, but I have assumed that most people are, so the first of several is given in figure 1 (page 21), which summarises the ages and stages of primary education. The ages are shown on the left, from 2:0 (two years no months)—the lowest age of eligibility for nursery school, right up to 12:0 (twelve years no months)—the normal upper limit for transfer to secondary education.* The width of the diagram at any point represents very roughly the number of children of a given age who are in school; thus, very few children aged 3:0 are in school, but virtually all children aged 6:0.

The sloping lines indicate age at certain fixed points in the year —usually at the beginning of September, the start of the educational year.[1]† They embody a device for denoting children's ages by year-group—what may be called the 'plus concept'. For example, everyone is familiar with the term 'eleven plus' for the age at which children normally transfer to secondary education. These children can be thought of as strung out along the line labelled 'eleven plus' in the diagram, their ages at the beginning of September ranging from 11:0 to a day short of 12:0. Similarly, the seven-plus year-group consists of children, strung out along the sloping line so labelled, who at the beginning of September would be between 7:0 and a day short of 8:0, and just entering the junior school. Indeed, throughout the first

---

* This upper limit of 12:0 (strictly one day short of this) is true of all Local Education Authorities (LEAs) transferring children to secondary school at the traditional age of eleven plus. Some authorities, however, now make this transfer at twelve plus or thirteen plus.

† Superior figures throughout the book refer to notes at the end of the chapters.

between 5:0 and 5:4—which is one reason for the overlap indicated in the diagram between the age-spans of nursery and infant education.

Many nursery schools and classes nowadays are half-time—the teacher has one group, usually of up to thirty, in the morning, and a different group in the afternoon. So the qualified nursery teacher and her nursery assistant work a full day, but any particular child only attends for the morning or the afternoon session. The first experiments in half-time nursery education were begun in London and Bristol in the early 'fifties, at the suggestion of the Central Advisory Council for Education. Originally, the main reason for the experiment was that it would enable more children to have the advantages of nursery education, despite the shortage of teachers: in other words, that half a loaf is better than no bread. It was soon realised, however, that for many children, half a loaf, of the same quality, is better than a whole loaf; very often a child makes a better transition from home to school if at first he spends half the day in school and half the day with his mother. The conviction that this is the right initial pattern of schooling for most young children has spread rapidly since these first experiments; it will be examined more fully in later chapters, since it is an essential part of the thesis of this book. It is now true of Inner London, and increasingly in other areas, that more than half the children receiving nursery education attend only half-time. This trend is likely to continue, though one hopes that some full-time nursery education will always be retained for those who really need it.

It was said earlier that nursery education, unlike the other two stages, is 'voluntary'—in the sense that school attendance at this age is not required by law. It is *not* voluntary in the sense of all parents having a free choice whether and at what age their children should have nursery education. Far from it, and for two reasons: firstly, because the *total number* of nursery places falls far below the total demand; secondly, because the *distribution* of nursery provision is very patchy. There are some neighbourhoods where most children whose parents wish it can find a place, and others where there may be no provision at all within a reasonable journey from a child's home, and where in any case those children living nearer the school will be given priority. There are often long waiting-lists; then children of middle-class parents who 'know the ropes' and have the forethought to put their children's names down early may get in, though others may stand in greater need.

The overall shortage of nursery places stems from the general shortage of teachers of young children and from the priority given to other demands on scarce money, manpower and building resources. For these reasons, the Ministry of Education issued in May 1960 a circular (Circular 8/60) limiting the power of a local authority to increase the number of nursery places* beyond those provided in January 1957. There have since been some minor relaxations of this limitation, for example, to enable a new nursery class to be opened where it could be shown that a sufficient number of mothers who had been teachers would be released thereby to return to teaching. Some local authorities, eager to achieve at least a limited expansion of nursery education, have been quick to take advantage of these relaxations; others, more niggardly of expenditure on education, have made less use of them. So these slight easements of the strict control may even have increased the patchiness of nursery provision. A more important recent development has been the *Urban Aid Programme*, under which the government has provided, among other things, for some expansion of nursery education in the 'educational priority areas' of big cities. This is a welcome advance, stemming from the Plowden principle of 'positive discrimination' in favour of the socially deprived.

Despite these relaxations and developments, experience of nursery education in grant-aided schools is still only available to about one child in nine (see page 72). This meagre provision is indicated in figure 1 on page 21 by the narrow triangles, gradually expanding from two to five, which represent it. And whatever one may think about financial and building priorities, there is something to be said for the argument that, while *teachers* are

---

* In strict accuracy, the limitation was on the number of children, whether in nursery or in infant classes, who were not yet rising-five.

scarce, the needs of infants, who *must* be in school, should come before those of nursery children, who need not be. Under present arrangements, this choice is inescapable in respect of the one thing which takes time to expand—teaching manpower. I say 'under present arrangements' since we shall see later that one of the merits of the *London Plan* is the negligible demand it makes for additional teachers, so that as we get them they will remain available for a general improvement in teaching-staff standards.

THE INFANT STAGE

So much, for the moment, for the nursery stage. Let us go on to see what happens to the vast majority of children who begin their schooling at the infant stage. We come back, I fear, to figure 1 and to some unavoidable technical terms, which will be much needed in later chapters.

We usually think of the age of compulsory school attendance as five years. But the law does not require a child to be in school until the beginning of the term *after* he becomes five. Only then is he what we call a *statutory-five*—a five-year-old 'within the meaning of the Act'. For example, a child who becomes five in mid-January does not become a statutory-five till after the Easter holiday, and he might have to wait till then before he can get into school. So the age of *compulsory* school attendance is not an absolutely precise age, but rather a range, varying from 5:0 up to about 5:4, according to the individual child's birthday and how this relates to school terms and the local pressure on school places. This range is indicated in figure 1. So this gives us one important technical term—*statutory-fives*—children who were already five before a term began.

Now, although some children have to wait till well beyond their fifth birthday before they get into school, a good many are admitted during the term in which they become five, usually at the beginning of that term, when they may be anything from 4:8 to virtually 5:0. Children who become five in the course of a term are spoken of *throughout that term* as *rising-fives*. They are approaching five as term begins, but they are not yet five. Even if they turn five in the course of the first week, they are still spoken of as 'rising-fives', since they do not *have* to be in school, by law, till the beginning of the following term. So here is another important technical expression—*rising-fives*—children who become five in the course of the term in question.

In most local education authorities, the autumn rising-fives, children born between September and early January, are automatically admitted in September, and the staffing of the schools allows for this. This follows from the fact that the 'authorised staff' of a school containing infants is normally settled before the school year begins, on the basis of the number of children of five and over it is expected to contain the following January. This number will include the autumn rising-fives who, by January, will all be statutory-fives. It is reasonable that provision for these children should be made in advance, so that the head teacher can plan her staffing and class organisation for the whole year.★ So this means that the autumn rising-fives, born from September to early January, are all normally able to enter school in September, at ages ranging from 4:8 to almost 5:0. I say 'normally' since there are some local authority areas where, owing to pressure on school places, they cannot be admitted. Moreover, these autumn-born children are not obliged to enter school in September, not being yet of statutory school age. Nevertheless, most parents of autumn-born children take advantage of the places which in nearly all schools are available for all of them.

These autumn-born children can be seen in figure 1 to enter school along the short sloping line, labelled 'Sept.', at the bottom right of the diagram. And if you count up the years in the diagram, you will see that they have a full three years of infant schooling and seven years of primary schooling altogether.

The spring and summer-born children are less fortunate, and their fate less certain. They are only admitted as rising-fives—in January for the spring-born and after Easter for the summer-born —if there is then room in a class already authorised for statutory-

★ As will appear presently, some schools, however, need to be allowed an additional infant class in the summer term.

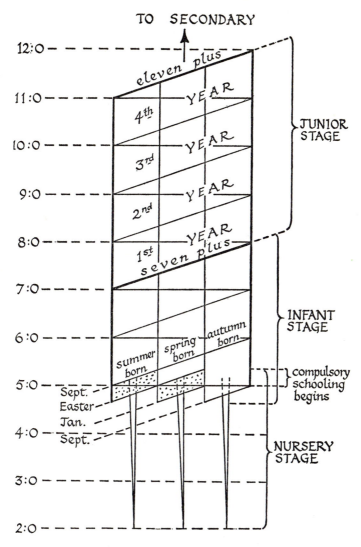

Figure 1. Primary education: a flow diagram

fives. Otherwise, they have to wait till the following term, when they themselves will be statutory-fives and must be admitted. The dotted parallelograms in figure 1 are intended to indicate this uncertainty whether a particular spring-born or summer-born child can come in as a rising-five or must wait till the following term. For example, a spring-born child may be admitted as a rising-five in January and have then two years and two terms of infant schooling. But he may have to wait till after Easter, and so have only two years and a term. On average, taking England and Wales as a whole, this is the fate of perhaps a quarter★ of the spring-born. Sometimes a special summer-term class has to be formed for these spring-born children who, as statutory-fives, have then, by law, to be admitted.

As to the summer-born, only about a third★ of them, on average, can be admitted as rising-fives after Easter, and so have two years and a term of infant schooling. The remaining two-thirds have to wait till September, and it will be clear from the diagram that they then have only two years of infant schooling, and six years of primary schooling altogether.

The handicapping of the summer-born

This numerical analysis,[2] tedious though it is, is important since it demonstrates the reasons why length of infant schooling depends on when a child's birthday happens to come. This is especially important for the summer-born child who gets, as we have seen, at most two years and a term of infant schooling, and more usually only two years. And this *handicapping of the summer-born* is in fact a double or triple handicap. Not only does the child get a shorter infant schooling, but he is, throughout, young within his year-group. Moreover, if as Plowden suggested (paras. 360–64), seven plus is rather young for most children to transfer to the junior school, this will be true especially of the summer-born who are only just seven at the time of transfer. And throughout his junior-school life, the summer-born child may easily be underestimated. He is compared with other children in his year-group who have not only had longer infant schooling, but who are older within the year; so, unless the teacher keeps his age in mind, he may easily be thought duller. As we shall see presently, in our

★ The basis for these estimates is discussed on pages 116-7.

consideration of streaming, these handicaps may persist throughout the junior stage, and perhaps beyond. Any reform of school admission policy must find some way round this birthday lottery, which makes for inequality of opportunity at the very outset of schooling.

To some readers, the thought may perhaps occur that the birthday handicap and the whole pattern of admission and transfer that gives rise to it, are artificial situations arising merely from the preference of administrators for dealing with children in neat cohorts. Let us suppose, for example, that all children entered the infant school on their fifth birthdays, transferred to the juniors on their eighth birthdays, and to the secondary school on their twelfth birthdays, and that these admissions and transfers occurred day by day, whenever in the school year these anniversaries happened to come. Certainly, this would equalise the time spent by different children at the infant stage; it would also provide automatically for staggered entry and stability of staffing. But there would be very real difficulties later on which would most certainly *not* be just matters of administrative untidiness. For example, at the secondary stage, it would be very difficult to apply schemes of work and to arrange courses leading to public examinations, if children were entering secondary school day by day throughout the year. And even at the junior stage, there are certain positive educational advantages in children falling broadly into year-groups. This is no pseudo-problem, therefore, but one demanding all the ingenuity and understanding we can muster, to find the right solution.

THE JUNIOR STAGE

In most authorities, the junior stage continues to extend from 7+ to 11+, though as we shall see, some localities are adopting a different arrangement (page 33). With these exceptions, and the odd case of the child retained for some special reason for a term or two longer in the infants, children move on to the junior stage in September if they have reached the age of 7+ by then. So they have just four years at the junior stage. During this time, it is convenient for some purposes to think of children as 'first-year juniors', 'second-year juniors', and so on—though it needs to be remembered that there is virtually a year's difference in age between the youngest and the oldest children in a year-group.

Although the 'year-group' is to this extent artificial, it acquires a certain psychological reality as a result of the fixed dates for transfer: children of the same year-group look upon each other as contemporaries, since they come up from the infant school together and go on to the secondary school together. Most junior teachers, therefore, see some advantages in keeping juniors in classes of the same year-group where this is possible. In this way, the class community can remain as a continuing unit, year by year, and the simplicity of the arrangement helps teachers in keeping track of children's progress and in applying schemes of work.

All this is easy enough provided that the number of classes in the junior school is a multiple of four. Then you will have one class in each year-group, giving a four-class junior school; or two classes in each year-group, giving an eight-class junior school, or three classes in each year-group, giving a twelve-class junior school. A junior school as large as sixteen classes is rather rare. Often, however, the number of classes justified by the total roll, or which the accommodation permits, is not a simple multiple of four. Then, inevitably, some classes have children of more than one year-group. This matters less than it did, now that so much of children's learning is in small groups or as individuals, rather than through whole-class teaching. Indeed, some teachers of juniors favour some measure of vertical grouping (pages 42–5), in which an age-span of, say, two year-groups per class is deliberately organised—though such an arrangement has, perhaps, fewer merits and more disadvantages at the junior than at the infant stage.

STREAMING

We turn to a far more controversial aspect of junior organisation: grouping across a year-group by ability or attainment, or streaming as it is generally called. Forty years ago, it was taken for granted that if you had an eight-class junior school, two classes in each year-group, you would divide the children into an A class and a B class according to ability. In a twelve-class school you would have A, B, and C streams; and in a sixteen-class school, A, B, C, and D. At that time it seemed obvious sense to make each class as homogeneous for ability as the size of the school would allow. Nowadays, many teachers and educationists are less sure.* Their misgivings are highly relevant to the theme of this book, since there is reason to believe that the summer-born, with their double or triple handicap, find themselves more often than others in the lower streams.

Completely up-to-date information on the incidence of streaming in schools containing juniors in England and Wales is not available. The most recent large-scale survey was conducted in 1963 by the National Foundation for Educational Research† which elicited returns from 1 753 schools. Some 55 per cent were too small to stream at all, in that they contained four or fewer junior classes. Another 21 per cent were too small to stream completely, since they had from five to seven junior classes. They used a variety of methods of organisation, in most cases involving some differentiation of classes according to ability. The remaining 24 per cent were large enough to stream on traditional lines and the methods they employed distributed as follows:

Wholly streamed	*Streamed 2nd, 3rd and 4th years only*	*Streamed 3rd and 4th years only*	*Streamed 4th year only*	*Wholly non-streamed*	*Other methods*
50%	15%	4%	5%	6%	20%

* For a well-argued case against streaming, see B. Jackson, *Streaming: An Education System in Miniature*, (Routledge and Kegan Paul 1964). The NFER has issued a number of reports on its large-scale Streaming Research Project, of which the most important is J. C. Barker Lunn, *Streaming in the Primary School* (NFER 1970).

† J. C. Barker Lunn, 'The Effects of Streaming . . . Interim Report' (*New Research in Education*, Vol. 1, 1967).

Thus, even in 1963, although only 6 per cent of the schools which were large enough to stream fully were completely non-streamed, only 50 per cent were wholly streamed and the rest had some compromise arrangement. Almost certainly today, the proportion wholly non-streamed would be higher and only a minority would be entirely streamed.

The traditional case for streaming rests on the supposed greater efficiency of the teacher, faced with a class of limited range of ability; and in several ways there is little doubt that in such a class the teacher's task is easier. In whole-class lessons, it is easier to be sure that what is taught is within the comprehension of everyone. There is less need to use group methods in oral work. Even in individual work, it is easier to keep track of children's progress when the range is not wide. There is less switching of the teacher's mind, from the child who can barely read to the child who is fully capable of 'research' in the school library. Undoubtedly, the non-streamed class, if it is to be well taught, demands more effort of the teacher.

This is the traditional case for streaming, with the emphasis on the *teacher's* task. But a case is also made on more modern grounds, in terms of the children's reaction to each other in class work and of their social and emotional life. Many teachers think that the bright child works harder in an A class, that able children gain stimulus from each other, and that there may not be enough of them in a non-streamed class to give this stimulus. It is also said that in a non-streamed class the able children may get impatient of the less able, who hold things up; alternatively, the able children may tend to rest on their laurels. Again, some teachers think that the less able child in a non-streamed class may get discouraged, feel unsure of himself, and be diffident of taking part in oral lessons for fear of becoming a laughing-stock. He suffers, it is thought, from all sorts of daily pin-pricks: using a different mathematics book, getting poor marks, day after day, in tests, and so on. Moreover, in a C class, it is claimed, such children have opportunities for leadership and achievement which might be denied them in a non-streamed class.

But an equally varied case is made by the opponents of streaming. They base their case, firstly, on the view that a non-streamed class is a more natural community, whose very diversity is a merit. Indeed, it is said that its diversity may enforce good teaching by compelling the teacher to attend to individuals, instead of thinking of the class as a homogeneous whole, which even an A class is not. In other words, it is argued that non-streaming *makes* good teachers. If the teacher is moderately good to start with, this may well be so; he may become really good in response to the challenge. Secondly, it is claimed that in non-streamed schools the whole atmosphere is sweeter and more relaxed, that within the non-streamed classes the able children show great willingness to help the less able, and that they join together more freely in out-of-school activities. Thirdly, it is thought that the less able children do better in non-streamed classes; that they are stimulated, not discouraged, by the presence of the brighter children. It is said that there may often be a secondary effect here, transmitted through the parents; the parents of average and below-average children in a streamed school may often, it is said, be discouraged and disenchanted with the school where their children are labelled as B or C, and this discouragement affects the children. This does not happen in a non-streamed school. Lastly, many heads of non-streamed schools claim that the brighter children do just as well in non-streamed classes. Some would concede that the last inch or two of speed in mechanical arithmetic may be less readily obtainable from the brightest children in a non-streamed class than in a good A class, and that it is less easy to train children like little race-horses in a non-streamed school. But they would say that if this is so and if it matters, the better atmosphere of the school more than compensates.

This is the kind of difference of opinion that one finds among competent and devoted head teachers on this question. But there are some areas of common ground. Undoubtedly, the non-streamed class demands more of the teacher. To the good teacher it can be more interesting and varied; with the weak or inexperienced teacher it can make for failure. So much depends on staff. Much also depends on the size of classes; as classes get smaller, non-streaming is easier to work successfully. Again, non-streaming demands really good group and individual ways of working; these are desirable in all classes; they are especially necessary in non-streamed classes. Indeed, one reason why non-streaming and other progressive methods often go together is that both accord with an emphasis on the individual child rather than on the class as a unit, taught in lock-step. Finally, everyone would agree that the teacher's attitude is fundamental. Dull children will be discouraged, whether in a C class or in a C group in a non-streamed class, if the teacher looks down on them and is for ever making invidious comparisons. Or, as some teachers still do, tells a visitor in a stage whisper: 'Of course, this is a C class—they're very dull', and then perhaps points to the boy in the front row: 'He's ESN—shouldn't be here at all!' No child is so dull that he does not feel such remarks like a blow in the face.

Such are the varied views of teachers on this controversial question. Some of them remain matters of opinion, but the NFER studies have somewhat extended the area in which opinion gives way to fact. Perhaps their most important finding was a negative one: that there was no difference at all in the average attainment gains of children of comparable ability in streamed and non-streamed schools—and this despite the fact that many of the teachers in the non-streamed schools were still using methods more appropriate to a streamed situation. One can conclude that to unstream a school entails little risk to attainment; indeed, it might lead to better attainment as all teachers come to accept non-streaming and adapt their methods accordingly. The NFER findings also lend some support to the belief that children's attitudes to their class and school and their relationship with teachers are better in non-streamed schools, though this finding applies chiefly to the average and below-average children when these are taught by teachers sympathetic to non-streaming.

There seems little doubt that the trend towards unstreaming of junior schools will continue, now that teachers can be assured that the risks to children's attainment are minimal. As head teachers have gained confidence in this belief, more and more have begun to unstream their junior classes 'from the bottom', beginning with the first-year juniors, then letting these go up unstreamed into the second year, and so on. Many will thus gain the confidence to take it all the way. Even then, some may wish to retain a small 'opportunity class' for slow learners, under a teacher with special gifts. Throughout this process, close consultation with staff is essential, for one thing has emerged clearly from recent studies: that the effective use of a non-streamed organisation depends greatly on class teachers' believing in it.

We turn finally to the relationship between streaming and the handicapping of the summer-born. The NFER study (Barker Lunn 1970)* confirms the earlier evidence of Jackson and others that a higher proportion of the summer-born than of children born at other times tend to be placed in the lower streams of a streamed school. Conversely, a higher proportion of the autumn-born, mostly with three full years of infant schooling, are apt to be found in the A stream. It seems clear that the handicap in attainment suffered by many summer-born children—through their shorter infant schooling and through being young within the year—can have an influence on their allocation to a class when they enter a streamed junior school. Yet, when this happens, it is a quite arbitrary consequence of date of birth.

This might not matter very much if one could be sure that a fairly able child, whose attainment was at first limited for these reasons, might still have every chance to forge ahead in his lower-stream class and eventually be 'up-graded'. However, this may not often happen. For one thing, the amount of transfer, year by year, between streams is usually quite small; as a rule it is too little even to allow for the variation in intelligence year by year, let alone to correct initial errors of placing. So, many children, once placed in the C stream, are on a conveyor belt, with little hope of escape. Secondly, many educationists believe that there is a tendency in a streamed school towards what has been called 'stereotyping' or 'the self-fulfilling prophecy', the A's becoming more A, the B's more B, and the C's more C in the course of their junior-school life.

Whether this is generally true is still a little uncertain, and the NFER findings on this point are not clear-cut. Moreover, some

* See footnote on page 25.

earlier findings indicating the existence of stereotyping could be accounted for if the A classes often got the best teachers; they might not be due to the effects of streaming in itself. However, what the NFER did show quite clearly was that children who are 'wrongly placed', in a class either above or below their ability, tend to take on the characteristics of the class in which they are. This could affect the summer-born child. The slower pace of a C class, and the discouragement of being in it, may damp down the progress of potentially able children, who are only there through their birthday handicap, so that they take on many of the characteristics of their fellows who are genuine slow learners. If so, this is a tragic consequence of our present admission arrangements, adding greatly to the many reasons for looking at them afresh.

Meanwhile, even those schools which still retain some streaming could do much to meet the problems of the summer-born if they would at least unstream their first and second-year classes. As long ago as 1957, Vernon* and his collaborators expressed the view that 'Up to at least nine years we see no real case for any streaming.' It could mean much to many summer-born children if, at just seven, and after only two years of infant schooling, they entered an unstreamed junior class and had at any rate a couple of years to find their feet—without any conveyor belt to carry them to a pre-determined destination.

DIFFERING PATTERNS

School organisation in this country is never simple and it would be misleading to complete this account of primary organisation without a brief mention of certain complications.

For the sake of simplicity, I have spoken so far of 'the infant school' or 'the junior school' as if they were always separate departments, each under its own head teacher. This is often the case, though even then, the departments usually share a building or at least a site. But, about as often, the infant and junior classes form a single junior-and-infant school under one head teacher.

* P. E. Vernon, (ed.) *Secondary School Selection* (Methuen 1957).

Indeed, in the country as a whole, there are rather more combined junior-and-infant schools than there are separate infant schools and separate junior schools added together. Nevertheless, the total number of pupils in combined schools is rather less than the total numbers in separate departments. This is because rural primary schools are often junior-and-infant schools and are often small. The same is true of many church schools serving small parishes. The actual figures* for maintained primary schools in England and Wales in January 1969 were as follows:

Type of organisation	Schools	Pupils
Infant only	5 540 (24·0%)	1 131 507 (23·5%)
Junior only	4 949 (21·5%)	1 509 227 (31·4%)
Junior-and-infant	12 543 (54·4%)	2 165 088 (45·0%)
All-age (primary and some secondary pupils)	22 (0·1%)	5 547 (0·1%)

In addition, there were 15 middle schools with 4 750 pupils.

A combined junior-and-infant school has some advantages. It can—though it does not always—help teachers to see primary education as a whole. It can—though it does not always—lead to flexibility in the use of staff. For example, an infant teacher may take her class up into the junior stage, often with great benefit to continuity of learning; a junior music expert may give a top infant class the benefit of his skill; an infant teacher who is expert in French may have the refreshment of taking a junior class in her subject for several short lessons each week; and so on. All this is excellent, and there is the further social advantage of a mixed staff-room, where a separate infant school would normally have women only. For the children, there can be complete continuity, both of familiar surroundings and people and of schemes of work.†

Where, instead, there are two separate departments, a good deal of careful thought needs to be given (but is not always given) to making the transition from infants to juniors easy and secure.

* Adapted from: *Statistics of Education, 1969*, Vol. 1. (HMSO 1970).

† Regrettably, this opportunity for continuity in the curriculum is all too often missed, especially in the larger junior-and-infant school.

On the other hand, there is no doubt that most of the best developments in infant methods have emerged in separate infant departments under infant-trained headmistresses, and that the head of a junior-and-infant school may not be sufficiently skilled in infant work to give much help to his infant colleagues. Indeed, he may be so preoccupied with the juniors that the infants get a poor deal. Fortunately, this position is improving and there are now a fair number of head teachers of combined junior-and-infant schools—including some headmasters—with a good understanding of the infant stage. The question of size of school also comes into it. A sizeable primary school has some advantages, for example, in the number of posts carrying salary allowances, and in the variety of talents the staff may offer. On the other hand, a junior-and-infant school of more than about ten classes may be a rather overwhelming community for the younger infants to adjust to; and, if the neighbourhood has many social problems, there may well be too many children and parents for one head to know really well. In these circumstances it may well be that 'two heads are better than one'.

For these reasons, when local authorities plan new schools, they tend to plan one-form-entry junior-and-infant schools (three infant classes and four junior classes) when the catchment area is small, and two-form-entry, two-department schools (six infant classes and eight junior classes) when the catchment area is larger. In the latter case, the infant and junior departments have separate heads, so this variety in organisation has a further advantage: it provides suitable niches for teachers with the potentiality for headship, but with varying talents. Not all teachers who would make good heads would be well suited to lead a school covering the whole primary range; some would be excellent with infants, others with juniors, but not necessarily with both; yet their capacity for leadership should not be wasted. Our varied pattern can ensure that it is not.

Before leaving this problem, it is worth noting that in future the age-range of primary education may tend to become extended at both ends, adding greatly to the need for versatility in the head of a primary school with this extended range. Already some junior-and-infant schools have nursery classes attached; if nursery education is expanded on traditional lines, more will do so; if it is extended in the way suggested in this book, all junior-and-infant schools will in time include some provision for the nursery stage. At the upper end, changes are already in progress. Plowden suggested extending the age-range of the infant school to 8+ and re-naming it the first school, which would then feed a middle school with a range from 8+ to 12+. Some authorities have already adopted this arrangement, in some cases making the break between first and middle school at 9+ and that between middle and secondary school at 13+. So a combined primary school with nursery provision might then have an age-range from 3+ to 13+. As Plowden points out (para. 465) such a combined school would present considerable difficulties:

'Either the school community will be too large for the younger children or, if it is small enough for them, the staff will be few and may not give enough stimulus to the older children.'

It might be added that the head required to give good leadership over such a wide age-range would indeed need to be a paragon.*

THREE PROBLEMS

For the sake of completeness, in this general review of primary organisation, I have touched on many things, some of which cannot be pursued further in this book. For this reason it may be helpful to pick out three problems which have already emerged in the course of this account, and which will be explored much more fully in later chapters. The first is the problem of the transition from home to infant school—how can this be made

* One further complication in our primary organisation perhaps merits no more than a footnote: a few primary schools are not mixed. Thus, one may occasionally find a junior boys school, or a junior girls school, or even a junior-girls-and-infants school in which children start as mixed infants and then, when they reach the ripe age of seven, the boys are whipped away! Some of these single-sex primary schools have been very good indeed in their way, but they are survivals of a past age and, as opportunity offers, they tend to be amalgamated and disappear.

easier, even with our present admission arrangements, and the stresses and strains that many children suffer avoided? The second is the birthday handicap, the built-in inequality of opportunity which is inherent in our present admission policy. The third is the vital need to extend the provision for the nursery stage—to make it as thick on the ground as the infant provision. These are among the key problems which any long-term policy for primary education must help to solve. We shall consider the first of these in the next chapter.

NOT BY BREAD ALONE...

This chapter is about the *organisation* of primary schools, the framework of ages and stages within which they work. It says nothing about the spirit in which that work is done or the changes in methods that the years have brought. This is familiar ground to the professional, but there may be some readers—the interested parent, for example—who want to know more. Three[3] books, two short and one long, may meet this need. For those who want to know more about nursery education and the case for expanding it, Willem van der Eyken's short book *The Pre-school Years* (Penguin 1967) is admirable. It will be referred to more than once in later chapters. On infant and junior schools, John Blackie, formerly Chief Inspector at the Department of Education and Science, has written a book for parents and others which cannot be bettered (*Inside the Primary School*, HMSO 1967). And for those who want to pursue the problems of primary education in some depth, there is, of course, no substitute for the Plowden Report (HMSO 1967). Bulky though it is, it is so well written that the journey through it is a delight.

NOTES

1. In strictest accuracy, a child born on the first day of a term really belongs to the previous term-age-group. This follows from

the Family Law Reform Act 1969, Section 9, which came into force on 1 January 1970. It provides that the time at which a person attains a particular age expressed in years shall be the *commencement* of the relevant anniversary of the date of his birth. So a child whose fifth birthday is 1 September is regarded as becoming five at the *beginning* of that day, i.e. before term starts if 1 September is the first day of term. Unlike other September-born children, such a child is a statutory five-year-old throughout the autumn term. Similar considerations apply to children born on the first day of the spring term and of the summer term. This refinement of definition is important to administrators applying the law to the cases of particular children; for our purposes such perfect precision is hardly necessary.

2. Head teachers and administrators may be interested to consider in a little more detail the implications of the pattern of infant flow illustrated in figure 1 and discussed in this chapter.

Any infant school contains seven term-age-groups in September. This is obvious, if it is considered that it then contains three term-age-groups of 6+ children, three term-age-groups of 5+ children, and one term-age-group of autumn rising-fives. If it admits no rising-fives in January, it still contains seven term-age-groups in the spring term. In the summer term, however, the spring-born fives *must* be admitted, so the number of term-age-groups then rises to eight, plus any summer rising-fives who may be accepted.

The position is well illustrated by the case of a seven-class infant school, rising to eight classes in the summer term, but admitting no summer rising-fives. This is, numerically, the simplest possible case, since each class could, theoretically, consist of one term-age-group only. Such a school would send up to the juniors in September a year-group of exactly three classes and take in two classes of new entrants; one of these could consist of summer-born statutory-fives and the other of autumn rising-fives. Sending up three classes precisely, it would just fill a twelve-class junior school.

More generally, the rolls of the two departments are in balance if, in the summer term, the numbers of children *of statutory age* are in the ratio of 8 infants to 12 juniors. In the spring term, the balanced ratio would be 7:12. If, in a pair of departments, these proportions of infants of statutory age are exceeded, the junior roll will eventually rise, and the junior department may become over-full—unless there is a net outward migration from the neighbourhood which will hold numbers steady, despite the excessive output of the infant department. Such a 'time-bomb' in the roll is not uncommon in schools built since the War, in which the ratio of infant to junior accommodation is usually 9:12 rather than 8:12. For example, in small catchment areas it has been usual to build combined junior-and-infant schools of 7 classes, 3 infant to 4 junior, and in larger catchment areas to provide two-department schools in which 6 infant classes feed 8 junior classes. In the latter case, if the school is popular, the infant head may be tempted to fill up all her classes by the summer term. If she does this entirely with children of statutory age, then the inevitable result will be that eventually the junior classes will be over-filled. It is a good general rule, therefore, to limit the *statutory age* infant roll in the summer to two-thirds of the maximum desirable junior roll. Unless this kind of control is exercised, it may become necessary in two or three years time to restrict the infant intake quite drastically, so that the large numbers of juniors can be accommodated. This may then set up an alternating cycle of bulge and slack, every few years, which leads to friction between departments, difficulties in organisation, and parental dissatisfaction.

3. Four, in fact, but only this brief mention is possible of Dr Tessa Blackstone's study *A Fair Start* (Allen Lane the Penguin Press, 1971) since it was published when this book was already in page proof. It will be found particularly valuable for its account of the history of nursery education up to 1965, and for its analysis of the factors, local and national, which have limited its expansion.

| From Home to Infant School

Transitions in education are of vital importance. Whether they are made with ease and confidence and the eager anticipation of a new challenge, or with anxiety and distress, can colour for a long time a child's response to his new environment. This is true whether we are thinking of the transition from home to school, from infants to juniors, from juniors to secondary, or indeed from school to work. Many teachers now realise this and do all they can to make transitions easy. In this chapter we shall be concerned still with our present pattern of admission to school and consider how it can be made easier for the vast majority of children who go straight from home to an infant class.

To understand how this can best be done, we need to see this transition as it must appear to a child of five or under. Till he goes to school, his whole life has been centred on his mother. Whether she is a good mother or an indifferent one, she is his mother, the source, from the day he was born, of his security and orientation. He may never have been away from her, or at least from both parents, for as long as a day. A day is a long time to a child of just five, lacking the experience of ordered time that school itself brings. When his mother leaves him on that first morning in school, he may feel very uncertain just when he will see her again. So this is the first main cause of distress to the five-year-old just starting school: parting from his main source of security, his mother, for a period which to him is indeterminate. Most children, no doubt, soon gain a sense of how long this period will be, but for some a shadow of anxiety must persist for some while, as to when she will return, if at all.

The trauma of parting from his mother coincides with another traumatic experience—of numbers and noise. He has been used to the four or five persons of a small family circle—his own and

37

perhaps a neighbour's. He enters a classroom to find up to forty children noisily occupied with their own concerns. They are too young and too occupied to take much trouble to welcome a new-comer and put him at ease. His teacher will do her best, but perhaps as many as thirty-nine others claim her urgent attention, and to him she is a new adult of whom at first he is shy. No wonder he may feel bewildered, frightened and alone—though he may not always show it.

The classroom group of up to forty is bad enough, but on occasions he may be subjected to six or seven times that number, at assembly, at dinner-time and, worst of all, at playtime, and in the playground before afternoon school. For in the playground there are not only large numbers of children, most of them bigger than he is, but they will often be rushing about, letting off steam. Even children who otherwise adjust fairly easily to school may find the playground a noisy nightmare in the first weeks.

Then there is the unfamiliar building, so unlike the small house or flat he knows. The lavatories seem a long way off and he is uneasy about finding his way there in time, managing there by himself, and finding his way back to the right door, when all look alike.

PREPARATION FOR SCHOOL

These are some of the sources of anxiety to which five-year-olds starting school have been subjected in the past. Setting these anxieties at rest entails realising that they fall into two groups, which reinforce each other. On the one hand, there is separation from the mother. Then the child, already anxious for this reason, is subjected to other stresses: large numbers, noise, strange adults, a large and bewildering building. Something can be done to reduce the impact of each of these, but better still is to find ways of avoiding a situation in which these two sources of anxiety— mother-deprivation and the unfamiliar—coincide. To a considerable extent this can be done and it is the principle behind many of the devices which good schools adopt for smoothing the transition from home to school.

The child can get to know the school and some of the teachers, *with* his mother, before she has to leave him there. It is best that there should be a number of occasions for doing this, for children cannot become *familiar* with strange surroundings in one go. If there are older brothers and sisters at the school, this is easy, since the younger child can often come with his mother when she brings the older ones to school. Sometimes she may want to stay for a little while to talk to a teacher and there may then be an opportunity for the younger child to visit a reception class and join in for a short while. If the school is vertically grouped (pages 42–5) this may indeed be the class which contains the older brother or sister and this will help the younger child to feel at home. Then there will be open days and other occasions when the parents come to see the work of the older children and, if the younger child can accompany them, this will add to his acquaintance with the school building and teachers and the large numbers of children.

For the only child or the eldest child, these natural opportunities for visits to school with his mother do not arise and other ways have to be found. Many parents nowadays bring their children to school in the term before they are to begin so that their names can be put down on the waiting list; the headmistress can make it known in the neighbourhood that this is desirable. Often she has toys in her room that the child can play with while she takes down his particulars and has a friendly talk with the mother. They may then be taken together to the reception classroom so that the child can see the children playing there, with the reassurance of his mother's presence, and perhaps himself join in for a while. If the teacher of this class is the one he will have next term, she can greet him by name and make him welcome. If not, he may be taken to meet the teacher he will have, who again should have been told his name so that she can greet him by it. Little children seem to attach great importance to adults' knowing their names and to get pleasure from their use, so this is a small thing over which it is worth while to take some trouble. This first visit, which can usefully be repeated, should not only be free from anxiety but associated with pleasurable feelings, and it is worth an effort to ensure that this is so.

At this first visit, the mother may ask the headmistress what she herself can do to prepare her child for school. Extending the child's experience and encouraging him to talk about it are certainly of more value than any attempt by the parents to prepare the child more directly for learning the basic skills. It is useful too if the mother can encourage the child to be self-reliant in practical matters by the time he starts school: able to dress and undress, tie bows and do up buttons, and manage by himself in the lavatory. He will be helped with these things in his first weeks in school, but it will mean much to his self-esteem and confidence if he can manage them himself.

THE FIRST DAY IN SCHOOL

If the child has been prepared for school in the ways that have been described, he will enter on his first day a place which is already known to him and associated in his mind with pleasure and interest and friendly people. But he still has to part company with his mother and adjust to a new routine, so it is important that the first day should go smoothly and give him the reassurance he will still need.

Until quite recently, the first day of term in an infant school could be a nightmare for children and teachers alike. In September there might be the equivalent of two classes of new children, some seventy or eighty of them, assembling in the hall during the first hour of the first day to be registered and allocated to classes. With them, of course, would be their mothers—and sometimes their grandmothers—most of them nervous, and some, like the children, tearful. The head teacher had to tackle much of this chaotic pandemonium single-handed, for her two reception-class teachers would soon be fully occupied with the youngsters handed over to them. Getting down the particulars of each child was about all that could be done; there was no leisure to see that the child was happily settled and occupied when the time came to part from his mother, or to make the mother really welcome and tell her something of the routine of the school.

Nowadays things are very different in all good primary schools and it is amazing to us now that the inhuman arrangements of the past persisted so long, when a little common sense and flexibility could have shown the answer. For one thing, it is now usual for particulars to have been taken the previous term. This not only saves a little time on the first day, but also makes it more of a social than a fact-finding occasion.

Secondly, most schools containing infants now adopt some form of *staggered admission*. Not all the new entrants are expected on the first morning of term; their entry is spread, by arrangement with the parents, over a period. Take the case of a reception class due to build up eventually to some thirty-five new children. On the first morning there might be no admissions while the rest of the school settles in and the teacher puts the finishing touches to her room, already largely prepared during a visit at the end of the holiday. Thereafter children could be admitted at the rate of two each session, perhaps with a break on the last day or two of each week to consolidate those so far admitted. In this way, before the end of the third week the class would be complete. Obviously this arrangement has many advantages. The headmistress can give her full attention to the few children and mothers appearing each session. There will be time for her to show children the lay-out of the building and to answer mothers' queries in an unhurried way. When he joins his class, the child is not overwhelmed by large numbers of children all as new as he is. If he is among the early admissions, the numbers in the class will be too few to be frightening. If he comes later, when numbers have built up, he will join a class in which most children have begun to settle down and know what is expected of them. The class teacher has only a few new children to get to know each day and can give these few special attention—unobtrusively—in their first day or two. They can also have the special care of the infant helper over such matters as visiting the lavatory and dressing and undressing. In many schools she will be asked to give a special eye to the reception classes at admission times, so the burden of giving particular attention to the few children who are completely new is not great.

It is important, of course, that staggered entry and the reasons for it should be fully understood and accepted by parents. Most parents are very willing to co-operate, even at some inconvenience, if they know about it well in advance and it is properly explained. This can be done at a meeting of new parents in the term before their children start school. The opportunity can be taken to tell parents a little about the work of the first year—perhaps on the basis of a short film illustrating modern infant methods. After the meeting may be a good time (over cups of tea) to arrange with individual parents when their children will start, fitting this in as far as possible with their own arrangements. Flexibility is the keynote and the headmistress will not try to adhere too rigidly to a preconceived pattern, such as that illustrated above, if a little give and take will achieve willing cooperation.

There is one further point to consider about staggered admission. In September at least, the children to be admitted will include both statutory-fives and rising-fives (see page 35). Strictly speaking, the statutory-fives are required by law to enter school at the very beginning of term; in practice, however, most authorities are prepared to overlook a delay of a few days because of the great advantages of staggered admission. Even so, it should perhaps be borne in mind that those summer-born children who enter as statutory-fives in September will only get two years in the infant school; if staggered admission entails much delay in starting school, this time is lost from an infant schooling which some think to be too short. Any such loss will be more than offset, for many children, by the ease with which they settle down. Nevertheless, it seems reasonable that the statutory-fives should be given some priority for early admission, other things being equal, and this can be borne in mind in arranging dates with parents.

VERTICAL GROUPING

This way of organising an infant school (sometimes called 'family grouping') is now quite widely used. Instead of children being grouped 'horizontally' by age, so that the lowest class contains only the youngest children, the classes are parallel, each with a wide age-range. This may be as wide as rising-five to rising-seven, so that the whole infant age-range is divided on vertical lines. Or there may be a compromise arrangement in which most of the classes are vertically-grouped, but the older children, who will go on to the juniors the following year, are in separate classes.

Vertical grouping is very relevant to our present discussion, since some of its chief advantages relate to ease of admission and adjustment to school. In a school with the traditional horizontal grouping, the separate admission classes will consist in September entirely or mainly of new entrants, with few children or none who know the ropes. In contrast, under vertical grouping, all or most classes can accept new entrants, so there will only be a small number of them in each; the class community is already a well-established going concern and the new children are soon assimilated to its ways of working. With so few new children to cope with, the teacher can get to know them quickly and ensure that they settle happily. She may get some help in this from the older children in the class, some of them perhaps nearly seven, who can be very protective towards the young newcomers. Then again, with a wide choice of classes accepting new entrants, it is easy for the head to fit the child to the teacher; for example, a child who is already known to be disturbed can be placed with a teacher who is experienced and sympathetic.

Vertical grouping has a further advantage in relation to admission. New entrants arriving later in the year can be placed in whichever class has room at that time, without other classes being disturbed. Under the traditional arrangement it is often necessary to make room for new children in the reception class by moving other children up to the next class, and this may entail a general 'shuffle-up' throughout the school if class rolls are to be kept reasonably equal. This can be disturbing to the children moved and to a lesser extent to the classes. Often, with horizontal grouping, it can only be avoided by keeping the reception classes small at first, so that they can absorb the later entrants, but this entails the older classes being larger than they need be in the first half of the year. There is less need, with vertical grouping, for staggered entry to be spread over several weeks; with the new entrants divided among a number of classes, there will not usually be more than about ten per class, and these can be assimilated in ones and twos each session during the first week.

It is clear that vertical grouping has considerable advantages in easing the way into school and its adherents would claim that it has several other merits. The protective relationship of the older to the younger children is valuable to the social development of the older ones and a source of security to the younger. Where materials and activities have to be provided for all ages and abilities, the less able or less mature older child can find what suits him and so can the bright and mature younger child. There is some gain in community spirit among the staff, since all or most are concerned with the whole or most of the infant age-range and see it as a whole, instead of having a proprietary attitude towards new entrants or top infants or middle infants as the only ones they want to teach. This also makes for flexibility in the use of staff, since all or most classes have the same wide age-range and are therefore equivalent. And even in the detail of teaching, some advantages are seen; for example, in reading, it may ease the teacher's task if only a few children at a time are at the stage when they need intensive help with phonics; these few form a manageable group who can be given this help while the rest of the class are getting on with other activities.

On the other hand, not all teachers can cope successfully with the diverse needs of a class ranging from the least able rising-fives to the ablest sevens—a mental-age range of perhaps six years. There are dangers that the youngest children will be neglected and aimless and the oldest and ablest insufficiently challenged. If space is limited, there may be problems about accommodating all the equipment needed for all ages and abilities. Ways of learning in which the whole class, if it is much of an age, can be profitably involved, are more difficult to use successfully in a class of wide age-range. For example, it may not be easy to adapt the occasional class centre of interest so that five-year-olds and seven-year-olds both get the most out of it in terms of the basic skills. It may also be sometimes necessary to re-group the classes for story or music or physical education if these collective activities are really to be suited to the age and experience of the children. Finally, it must be admitted that vertical grouping (like non-streaming) makes it rather more difficult for the teacher to keep tabs on progress, when the children in her class differ so very widely in their stage of attainment. The good and experienced teacher can manage this, with her practised facility in switching her mind; some young teachers—often a majority on an infant staff—may be less successful, so that some children stagnate when a little help at the right time would carry them forward.

For such reasons, although vertical grouping has had a considerable vogue among progressive head teachers, there are many who, after a careful weighing of pros and cons, have concluded that it is not suited to the circumstances of their schools. Others have adopted the compromise arrangement already mentioned, in which vertical grouping embraces the lower and middle infants but not the older ones. There is something to be said for this since, as we have seen, the most clear-cut advantages of vertical grouping are concerned with easing entry to school. Such a compromise also avoids the possibility that some children will have the same weak class teacher for the whole of their infant-school life.

THE FIRST WEEKS

We return from this important digression on vertical grouping to the child whose first day in school has been made easier in the ways described earlier. Much can still be done to continue to smooth his path during the first few weeks. Even though he has been familiarised with the school in advance, the other source of anxiety, parting with his mother for a whole day, remains. Sometimes in the first few days the mother may be able to stay with him for a while in the classroom until he has become absorbed in play and can part with her happily. Often she may be encouraged to come for him early, perhaps by afternoon playtime, so that, for a week or two, the long day without her is shortened. If she lives near enough and can arrange to take him home for his mid-day meal, this also will help to break the long day, and will spare him the ordeal, for some young children, of the noisy numbers at school dinner. Such measures may not be necessary for all new entrants, but they will be helpful to some.

For the reception class as a whole, some other small adjustments may ease the strain. For the first few days at least, it may be best if they do not join the whole school for morning assembly, but have their own quiet little service in the classroom with their teacher. In some schools, the reception classes have a separate playtime for the first few weeks, so that they get used to the playground before they meet the whole school playing there. Or the reception class teacher may go into the playground with her children, as well as the teacher on duty, so that her children feel the security of her presence.

THREE NEW VENTURES

I have mentioned altogether some dozens of small changes by which entry to school can be humanised. Individually, they are little things, but they add up to a civilised and imaginative approach to this fundamental change in a child's life. Recently, however, three new ideas have been tried out here and there, which are rather more radical, and perhaps foreshadow future developments.

1. *Half-time admission of rising-fives*

From 1962 onwards, Miss G. M. Clemens, then headmistress of Bellenden Infant School in Camberwell, had been trying out a new pattern of admission for the rising-fives, and a number of other infant heads in Inner London have since followed her lead. We have seen that the rising-fives of the autumn term will have three full years in the infant school (page 20), and they are not obliged by law to be in school till January. Miss Clemens thought that it would ease their transition to school if, at least for the first half of the term, they could be half-time, attending either morning or afternoon only, and with a choice whether the mid-day meal is taken at home or at school. The reasons were, of course, fully explained to parents in advance and it is encouraging that, in this mainly artisan neighbourhood, with many immigrants, it was quickly accepted as the normal practice of this school. The plan has several advantages. Firstly, it extends to the rising-fives of the infant school what we now realise is the right initial pattern, as a rule, for the child of nursery age—half the day at school and half the day with his mother. The shortened day also prevents the over-tiredness from which many children suffer in their first term of full-time school. The option of taking the mid-day meal at home avoids what for many children is an additional cause of strain.

Two other advantages are alternatives, depending on the way the school is organised. In a school of about seven classes, there may be the equivalent of two admission classes in September (page 35). Half or nearly half of these new children will often be statutory-fives who could not be admitted in the summer term; the rest will be rising-fives. If the rising-fives enter a separate class and attend at first only half-time, they will have the advantage at first of a small class, since only perhaps seventeen or eighteen children attend each session. This will add to the benefit of half-time attendance in easing their transition to school. Alternatively, the new children can be allocated between the admission classes so that both of them contain both rising-five and statutory-five children. If then it is arranged that the rising-fives all come only in the morning, the statutory-fives gain the advantage of a small class in the afternoons. Bear in mind that these are summer-born children with only two years of infant schooling. This is one way in which they can be given for a time, for half of each day, a more favourable pupil-teacher ratio to speed their progress. Either alternative has advantages and which is adopted may depend on local circumstances.

2. *Half-time attendance of summer rising-fives*

This is now being tried out in some schools in Inner London, for a quite different reason from those behind Miss Clemens' innovation. In the Inner London Education Authority (ILEA) at present little more than a quarter of the summer-born can be admitted as rising-fives in the summer term, so nearly three-quarters of the summer-born have only a bare two years of infant schooling. It seemed at first that there would be room for twice as many of them to benefit from an additional term of school experience if rising-fives attended only half-time in the summer term. In practice the over-all gain in numbers attending would not be quite double, since in some schools over 50 per cent of the summer rising-fives can already be accepted. It is too early to say how this proposal will work out. It was offered to Inner London head teachers as a practice which they were free to adopt if they wished, according to their circumstances. One factor which would certainly influence them would be the quality of the teacher or teachers available for the class or classes concerned, which would often contain some full-time and some part-time children. If an additional class had had to be authorised for the summer term (page 22), and this was to be in the hands of an indifferent supply teacher, it might be unwise to expect her to cope with perhaps 30 full-time children and as many as 20 part-timers, even though there would only be 10 of these in the morning and 10 in the afternoon. Still, as a very partial remedy for the ills of our present imperfect arrangements for the summer-born, the device merits consideration where the circumstances are right.

3. *The Southampton Scheme*

In November 1967, Dr J. J. B. Dempster, the Chief Education Officer for Southampton, reported to his Committee on the success of a scheme for pre-entry groups which had been operating in most Southampton schools containing infants for about two years—but in one school for twelve years. The scheme has also recently been offered for the consideration of Inner London head teachers, but it is too early to say how widely it will be adopted there and with what success. Dr Dempster certainly had no doubt about its value in Southampton schools. Children who will be entering school full-time in a given term are offered the opportunity to attend a pre-entry group in the school for half a day each week during the preceding term. The children may join existing classes which have places to spare; alternatively, the group may be taken as a whole by the head teacher or a part-time teacher, using a spare classroom if one is available, or sometimes a medical room, dining room or the hall. Accommodation is often the problem and, unless a room can be set aside, it must be difficult to prepare a good classroom environment for these children. Even so, a variety of play activities can be provided, and there can be opportunities for singing and story. In some of the larger infant schools, two or three different half-day groups each week are necessary to cope with the numbers. Often, virtually all the children due to enter the following term wish to come. At first this was not so, and some children most in need were missing the opportunity. However, some heads have been keen enough to visit the homes of children not yet coming to a pre-entry group and as a result of their efforts and the influence of parents spreading the good news, the percentages attending have steadily increased.

Some of the benefit to the children of this imaginative scheme lies, of course, in their becoming gradually accustomed to school as an exciting interesting place which they visit just for half a day each week. They get used to working in groups, to using the equipment sensibly, and they become accustomed to the large numbers of children and get to know the teachers and the school building. The teachers also get to know them, so that special problems, such as speech defects, can be investigated in advance. In at least one school, pre-school medical examinations have been arranged and found valuable.

But a good deal of the benefit to the children is thought to come from a close relationship between the school and the mother having been formed well in advance of the child's full-time entry. Parents are required to bring and collect their children and encouraged to stay until their children have gained enough confidence to be left happily. Dr Dempster goes on to say: 'More or less elaborate schemes of talks have been evolved by schools to introduce parents to the aims and methods of infant education.

. . . The parents have responded with gratitude and enthusiasm and some have given practical help to the schools.'

These three schemes provide only minor adjustments to the existing pattern for starting school, in the sense that they can all be operated within the law as it stands. Nevertheless, the first and third at least, of which we now have substantial experience, point clearly to the success of a *gradual* entry to school, beginning part-time. We may see them as pointers to the right pattern for the future.

HOME AND SCHOOL

Throughout this discussion, I have repeatedly mentioned the need for close links between school and parents. There are short-term and long-term reasons why these are particularly important when children start school. In the short-term, it is obvious that a child is most likely to settle happily in school if he can see that the teachers and his parents know and understand and trust each other. The long-term reasons go deeper. The National Survey,* conducted for Plowden, showed that the attitude of parents towards their child's primary school and their interest in his education there, formed the most potent single group of factors affecting the child's attainment—more important, indeed, than either the quality of the school or the circumstances of the home. So parental attitudes are all-important. But there is no more favourable time for establishing this good relationship than when children are just *starting* school. This can be an anxious time for parents as well as children, and if schools can take this opportunity to set parental minds at rest, they will often find parents most accessible and open to suggestion and the foundations of future good relations will then be laid.

Such good relations, well begun, still need to be maintained and developed. Fortunately, in most good schools containing infants the almost daily contact of many mothers (and some fathers) with the teachers is well-established. The traditional

* *Children and their Primary Schools*, Vol. 1, paras 90–101; Vol. 2, Appendix 4.

notice: 'No parents beyond this barrier' has rightly been pilloried by Plowden, but it has already become, in most schools, a thing of the past. Increasingly, parents are welcomed on an equal footing, not merely to chat in a friendly way with the teacher as they hand their children over but, in more and more schools, to come sometimes to join in the daily service, or even to help in various ways in the classroom. There is much that they can do—helping with cookery or needlework or handwork, mending toys, joining in educational visits or the journey to the swimming bath, and even, for some fathers on night shift, taking the seven-year-old boys for football. Head teachers with much experience of using parents in this way have said that there are *no* parents who are willing to help for whom a useful job cannot be found. All this is a positive help to the teachers; what is more important is the involvement of the parents in the school and the effect of this on the children. One head has described the extraordinary, and rapid, way in which those children whose parents are helping in her school have blossomed in their work with, as she put it, 'a great burst of warmth and pleasure'. As Plowden (para. 129) sums it up:

'It has long been recognised that education is concerned with the whole man; henceforth it must be concerned with the whole family.'

CHAPTER 3   Before the Infant School

In the last chapter we looked at some of the ways of smoothing the transition from home to full-time infant schooling. While nursery education continues to be restricted to a minority, this is still a fairly abrupt transition most children must make. It happens, as we have seen, at any time between the ages of 4:8 and 5:4— dependent on local conditions, the child's birthday and, within the limits set by these, the parents' wishes. There are exceptions: in some areas of Wales and a few in England, for example, some children may be admitted to infant classes at about 4½ or even earlier. Nevertheless, taking England and Wales as a whole, the normal range of ages for admission to an infant class is 4:8 to 5:4, with the average at about 4:11.

For many children, it can be argued that this is a little young for them to begin full-time schooling. As we have seen in the last chapter, there is at first the anxiety of being away from mother for a whole day, and the various stresses associated with large numbers and an unfamiliar building and routine. All this wears off in time; and it can be argued that there would still be initial sources of strain, even if children started school at a later age. Nevertheless, it is broadly true that the younger the child, the greater will be the stress of a whole day in the whirl of activity of a class of up to forty. Admittedly, among the varied activities and in the permissive atmosphere of a good infant class, there are opportunities for some children to withdraw for a while for a little peace and quiet; but not all who need this will have the independence to use these opportunities. It is not surprising, therefore, that a fair proportion of children show signs of strain, during their first term in school, before the afternoon session is over. This common observation of infant teachers was confirmed by Plowden.* Moreover, in some children, signs of weariness are not always observable in the classroom; they stick it out there, responding manfully to the stimulus of the teacher, and then collapse into near-exhaustion when they get home.† In such cases, mothers can judge better than teachers. Of course, there is wide variation; some children of just five can take a full day in school and still have energy to spare. But this is half the point, that children vary. We have geared our curriculum and methods to the individual, but not our admission arrangements. That is partly what this book is about.

For many children, then, some slight deferment of the legal age for compulsory full-time schooling might have positive educational advantages. But I shall also advocate the urgent implementation of the large extension of nursery education which, for half a century or so, has received lip-service from educationists, governments and acts of parliament. There is no contradiction between these two propositions: that full-time infant schooling should begin a little later, but nursery education mainly half-time, be available to all whose parents wish it. Both are educationally right and, as we shall see later, the first could make the second possible within a few years. In effect, what is proposed is that starting school should no longer be the abrupt and arbitrary transition which I described on page 40, but a gradual introduction to school experience, extended for most children over a year or more, and beginning for many much earlier than at present, and that the whole process should be geared to the needs of the individual child.

PRESENT PROVISION FOR THE UNDER FIVES

Let us look then at the case for an extension of the present pro-

* In the course of the National Survey undertaken for Plowden (HMSO 1967) (Vol. 2, Appendix 6), a small study was made of 255 children in their first term at school. About 45 per cent showed signs of tiredness towards the end of the afternoon session, though only 4 per cent were rated as 'markedly tired'.

† See K. Hartley, 'Exhausted Infants' (*Where*, No. 25, 1966).

vision for children before the infant stage and, to begin with, at what is now available both in education and care.

This is easier said than done, as anyone who has tried to compile statistics of pre-school provision will testify. For one thing, the official statistics* have hitherto been provided by three departments, the Department of Education and Science (DES), the Home Office, and the Department of Health and Social Security, and refer to different dates in the year—which limits the precision of any combined statistics. Secondly, many of the official statistics require interpretation and sometimes adjustment if they are to be completely meaningful; for example, some categories cover what are, in fact, very different types of provision. Thirdly, official statistics take time to compile and may be, at times, two years or more out-of-date; where changes are rapid, as in the recent expansion of playgroups, the official figures give a most imperfect guide to the current situation.

For these reasons and others I shall not try to summarise the numbers of children receiving various forms of pre-school education or care in a neat table related to a single date. Any such table would need to be hedged about with footnotes and explanations and even then could be misleading. Instead, I shall give in the following pages a descriptive account of each type of pre-school education or care, with an indication of the number of children benefiting from it, based on the latest official sources and more recent data if available. As a rule I shall relegate to numbered notes at the end of the chapter the sources of these figures and particulars of the adjustments to them it is sometimes necessary

* Those who wish to pursue the statistics further may refer to the statistical reports of the three departments, issued annually. The most recent issues are DES: *Statistics of Education 1969, Vol. 1. Schools;* Home Office: *Children in Care in England and Wales, March 1969;* and Department of Health and Social Security; *Annual Report, 1969* (all three, HMSO 1970). Elspeth Howe's well-documented pamphlet *Under Five* (Conservative Political Centre 1966) provided an important review, up to 1964, of the provision for the education and care of children of nursery age. The Plowden Report attempted in Tables 4 and 5 to summarise, mostly for England only, the pre-school provision in 1965. Finally, a valuable review of the provision for the care of children under five is contained in S. Yudkin, *0–5: A Report on the Care of Pre-school Children* (Allen and Unwin for the National Society of Children's Nurseries 1967).

to make. In this way the more general reader will be spared the tedium of numerical detail which, however, the specialist can check if he wishes. At the end of the road, we shall know something in qualitative terms about the various kinds of provision. We shall also be able to do some adding up, so as to estimate—perhaps with rather greater completeness than has hitherto been attempted—the number of children in all for whom some form of nursery education is now provided.

The total child population[1] aged two to four inclusive in England and Wales amounted in January 1969 to 2 524 000, i.e. about 840 000 on average in each of the three year-groups. This grand total of some $2\frac{1}{2}$ million children of two, three and four is the upper limit of the pre-school population we need to consider, since no one has ever suggested that nursery education is appropriate to children under two. However, as we shall see, some forms of *care* (rather than education) are provided for children under two, as well as for older children, and we shall consider these in their place.

In what follows, for want of a better classification, I shall group the various kinds of pre-school provision under the three government departments which have hitherto recorded the numbers served. The numbers were recorded in January 1969 for the DES, in March 1969 for the Home Office, and in December 1969 for the Department of Health and Social Security.

1. Department of Education and Science

(i) *Nursery classes in maintained* primary schools.* In January 1969, there were 243 251 children aged two to four, full-time or part-time, in maintained primary schools.[2] About 93 per cent of these were four-year-olds, and in fact the majority of them would have

---

* Since many people are confused over the use of this term, it may be well to state that a 'maintained school' is simply one maintained by a local education authority. It may be a 'county school', both built and maintained by the LEA, or a 'voluntary school' originally provided, e.g. by a church. 'Direct grant schools' are maintained by grants direct from the exchequer, and 'independent schools' are not supported by public funds. The term 'grant-aided schools' refers to maintained and direct grant schools taken together.

been rising-fives who had only just entered infant classes in time for the January count. These rising-fives should not therefore be included when we are trying to estimate the scale of nursery provision. However, the 243 251 would also include a good many children attending authorised nursery classes attached to maintained primary schools.[3] As explained in note 3, this number cannot be stated precisely, but may be of the order of 60 000; the majority would be aged four. Over a third of them would be attending part-time.

(ii) *Children of nursery age in infant classes*. Forty years ago it was quite common for children who were barely four to be admitted full-time into the large infant classes of those days, if there was room. It was gradually realised that these 'baby rooms' provided unsuitable conditions for very young children, and this, together with pressure on accommodation, made this once widespread practice less common. However, a fair number of children in Wales, and in a few authorities in England, may still be admitted to an infant class before they are rising-five. In some other authorities, but very rarely, the odd child may be admitted before he is rising-five if there are quite exceptional difficulties in the home which this would help to solve. It is impossible to estimate at all precisely the total number of these children of nursery age in infant classes, but a very rough calculation[4] suggests that it might be of the order of 10 000. They will, of course, be included in the total, already given, of children aged two to four in maintained primary schools. Are we to consider such children as receiving a form of nursery education? Certainly not in the fullest sense, since they will not usually be in rooms as spacious as those reserved for nursery classes, and the teacher (usually infant-trained) will not, as a rule, have the help of a trained nursery assistant. Even so, infant teaching is now so concerned with the individual child, that we may assume that infant teachers with some of these younger children in their classes will do their very best to provide for them activities suited to their age. With a good teacher, they may gain stimulus from their contact with five- and six-year olds in what is, in effect, a family-grouped situation.

(iii) *Maintained nursery schools*. In January 1969 there were 32 240 pupils in maintained nursery schools, which are dealt with separately in official statistics from other maintained primary schools.[5] Of the total, 46·7 per cent were part-time, and there were 4·7 per cent aged two, 42·1 per cent aged three, 52·2 per cent aged four, and 1 per cent of five or over. The actual number aged two to four was 31 936.

(iv) *Other grant-aided schools*.[6] Small numbers of children aged two to four are found in other types of grant-aided schools, for example in the few direct grant nursery schools, in preparatory departments of direct grant grammar schools, and in special schools, whether maintained or direct grant. The total number of children aged two to four was 2 874, but it is likely that some hundreds had just entered as rising-fives, leaving perhaps 2 500 receiving a form of nursery education. In the direct grant nursery schools this will have been of high quality; in the others it will have varied, but the aim will have been to provide education suited to children of nursery age.

These four categories form the hard core of education for children of nursery age—that which is provided in maintained or other grant-aided schools. If we add it all up, we find that, to the nearest thousand, it comes to 104 000 children, which is 4·16 per cent of the total number aged two to four in the child population.

(v) *Independent or private schools*.[7] If such an institution has more than five children of five years or over it counts as a 'school' and is included in the statistics of the DES. (Otherwise it is regarded as a 'private nursery' and falls for statistical purposes under the Department of Health and Social Security). In January 1969, independent or private schools included in the education statistics contained 31 638 children aged two to four, of whom 15 010 attended part-time. Of the total, 29 per cent were in schools 'recognised as efficient' and the rest in 'other independent schools'. At the time of the January count, 22 689 of the children were aged four, but we cannot tell how many of these were in fact rising-fives who had just started school when the count was made. Perhaps, therefore, we should round the total figure down to about 30 000 children aged two to four receiving what was intended to be a course suitable to children of nursery age.

How far, in fact, such an intention will have been realised in these independent schools will vary a good deal. Some independent schools catering mainly for nursery children can be quite as good as those maintained by local authorities. On the other hand, some independent schools mainly for older children may provide something of a travesty of nursery education for the relatively few children of nursery age in an infant class. No doubt standards will gradually be raised as Her Majesty's Inspectors are able to give increasing time to the inspection of independent schools and as an increasing number are included in the 'recognised as efficient' category.

However, giving the independent schools the benefit of the doubt, we now arrive at a total of some 134 000 children aged two to four inclusive who were receiving what was intended to be nursery education in schools covered by the *Statistics of Education*. This is 5·31 per cent of the two-to-four age-group in the child population.

We now enter a far more dubious territory in which it is often difficult to say what is 'education' and what is merely 'care'. We begin with the fairly small number of children aged two to four recorded hitherto in the statistics compiled by the Home Office.

2. *Home Office* [8]

It is sometimes necessary, unfortunately, for young children to be cared for away from their families, often only for a short period at a time of family crisis.* The care is provided for either by local authorities or by charities such as Dr Barnardo's Homes. The children may be in residential establishments or boarded out with selected foster parents. On 31 March 1969, the number 'aged 2 but not of compulsory school age' so provided for was 9 336. Yudkin (see page 54) gives some distressing case histories illustra-

---

* M. L. Kellmer Pringle, *Deprivation and Education* (Longmans 1965) contains an excellent series of research studies mainly of children in care.

tive of the 'private fostering' which also occurs; the number of children involved cannot be estimated.

Though some residential nurseries may provide a form of nursery education, the vast majority of children in care (and certainly those with foster parents) will be receiving only 'care'. I therefore propose to omit them from my total in nursery education, especially as, for very many of them, their stay is short. In January 1971 responsibility for the statistics of children in care was transferred from the Home Office to the Department of Health and Social Security.

3. *Department of Health and Social Security*

Four main kinds of provision for the care (and sometimes the education) of young children have hitherto been covered by the statistics of this department: (i) day nurseries, (ii) registered child minders, (iii) private nurseries and (iv) playgroups.

(i) *Day nurseries* are provided mainly by local health authorities, but occasionally for children of staff by hospitals or factories. Apart from assistants and students, they are staffed either by qualified nurses or, more often, by women holding the certificate of the National Nursery Examination Board (NNEB). Day nurseries originally came into being not to provide, like a nursery school, for the education of young children, but to care for the physical health and, so far as they can, the mental health of children whose mothers are unable to look after them during the day. Nevertheless, as Plowden says (para. 313) 'Day nurseries have made and are making a contribution towards the intellectual and emotional as well as the physical well-being of children. . . .' and the need for them to do this has recently been urged in an official circular. A child in a well-run day nursery must surely be acquiring some of the experience of other people, of materials and things, of sharing and of social play which nursery education provides. Even so, their main *aim* is not to provide education so, rather arbitrarily perhaps, we will not include them in our total of nursery education provision. Nevertheless, some account of them is necessary as part of our total picture of the facilities for children under school age.

Usually about a third of the children in a day nursery are under two and some may be as young as six months. To meet the needs of parents who are obliged to work full-time, day nurseries are usually open from about eight in the morning until five or after at night. Priority is usually given to children of mothers who are widowed or unmarried or separated, or those of widowers, or to children coming from homes which are unsatisfactory in various ways. Because of the shortage of places and the needs of priority groups where the parents are working full-time, children can very rarely be accepted who only need half-time care. Very occasionally children can be accepted where the economic need to work may be less pressing, but where the community urgently needs the mother's skill, for example, as a qualified teacher or nurse. There is normally a charge which may be as little as 10p or 15p a day where there is economic hardship, but rising in some areas to near a pound a day where the parents can afford it.

Day nurseries were expanded greatly during the Second World War in order to release mothers for essential war work and by September 1944 there was accommodation for 71 806 children. However, in 1945 the Ministry of Health laid down the principle (Circular 221/45) that:

'The right policy to pursue would be positively to discourage mothers of children under two from going out to work; to make provision for children between two and five by way of nursery schools and classes; and to regard day nurseries and daily guardians as supplements to meet the special needs . . . of children whose mothers are constrained by individual circumstances to go out to work, or whose home conditions are in themselves unsatisfactory from the health point of view, or whose mothers are incapable for some good reason of undertaking the full care of their children.'

The expansion of nursery education here anticipated did not materialise, but the day-nursery provision has been allowed to run down steadily ever since the Second World War, although the new Urban Aid Programme is producing a minor reversal of the trend, providing in its first two phases some 2 000 additional places in deprived urban areas. On 31 December 1969 (before these additional places became available) the total number of children[9] on the registers of day nurseries provided by local authorities and voluntary organisations was 22 030. We can reckon that about two-thirds of these, say 14 000, were aged two to four years. These figures are for England only.

The remainder of the officially-recognised provision for children under five comes under the Nurseries and Child Minders Regulation Act 1948, and it is at this point that it becomes very difficult to tell, simply from the official statistics, just what kinds of group we are dealing with and how many children are involved—let alone whether they can be thought of as receiving education or only care. The Act provides for registrations of two kinds, of *premises* and of *persons*. The italics (which are mine) in the following two quotations from the Act make the distinction clear:

'*Premises* . . . *other than premises wholly or mainly used as private dwellings*, where children are received to be looked after for the day or a substantial part* thereof . . .' These registrations therefore include private day nurseries of various kinds, providing care for the whole of a working day, but also a fair number of what are locally regarded as private nursery schools, and a much larger number of playgroups operating in halls rather than in private houses.

'*Persons* . . . who for reward *receive into their homes* children under the age of five to be looked after as aforesaid.' So these registrations will include child minders (see below) and playgroups operating in the homes of the supervisors. They may also include some small private nursery schools in private houses.

The official statistics[10] (for England only) are as follows for the three years 1967-9. They show *premises* on the left and *persons* on the right and, in brackets, the number of places provided:

* Under an amending clause in the Health Service and Public Health Act 1968, 'a substantial part' is defined as two hours or more.

at 31 December	No. of registered premises	No. of registered persons
1967	4 252 (106 115)	4 946 (41 727)
1968	5 670 (141 987)	5 672 (45 875)
1969	8 159 (196 100)	17 957 (69 055)

These figures are worth quoting as showing the rapid expansion of some kind of provision to meet a crying need. But what kind of provision? Of the 8 159 premises in 1969, 954 provided all-day care, i.e. they were private day nurseries. Of the remaining 7 000 or so, we cannot tell how many were playgroups and how many were examples of the 'little nursery school round the corner' familiar to middle-class mothers. Of the registered persons in the right-hand column in the table, some would be running playgroups in their own homes, with an educational aim; others would be child minders and no more. When it comes to the children themselves we are equally in the dark; we do not know, for example, how many were under two and how many aged two to four. Furthermore, one must realise that the table only shows *places*, not *children* on registers. Playgroups often have more children attending than they have registered places, since most children do not attend every session for which the playgroup is open.

No one, of course, can blame the Department of Health and Social Security for not making fine qualitative distinctions not provided for in the Act; nevertheless one realises that one is exploring an ocean less fully charted than that of the Department of Education and Science. So let us leave the uncertainties about numbers for the moment and see what else can be said about the three remaining types of provision covered by the health statistics.

(ii) *Child minders.* A fair number of mainly working-class children are looked after during the day by child minders. So that the conditions under which the children are cared for can be inspected and supervised, a child minder is required to register with the local authority if, for reward, she receives more than two children under five, not her relatives, and not belonging to the same family,

for 'a substantial part of the day'. Some child minders, often
called 'daily guardians', are retained by local authorities to provide
this service to children for whom the authority has some kind of
responsibility; but these are a minority. Though some local
authorities limit the number of children per minder to five, the
average number is said to be nearer eight (Yudkin 1967) of
whom perhaps five, on average, might be aged two to four.

There is no doubt that child minding is increasing. Moreover,
although it is an offence for a child minder not to seek registra-
tion, some through ignorance of the law, and some perhaps
deliberately, do not do so. In 1964, Howe (1966) estimated that
about 15 000 children aged two to four were cared for by registered child minders. Almost certainly this number has now
increased considerably; the number in the care of unregistered
child minders cannot, of course, be estimated. No doubt most
registered child minders are doing, according to their lights, a
reasonably conscientious job. Still, a child minder does not aim
to do more than the name implies; in her own interest, at the very
least, she will wish to keep the child happy as far as she can, and
she is required to keep him safe. She is not, like the day nursery,
expected to give a skilled eye to his health (other than avoiding
risks of infectious or contagious disease), let alone to provide
like a nursery school or class, for his educational needs.

(iii) *Private nurseries.* This term has sometimes been used to cover
all types of provision in 'premises' registered under the 1948 Act,
including playgroups where these are held other than in private
houses. Playgroups have now become such an important part of
the total provision that I shall treat them separately. Under
'private nurseries' as I am using the term we are therefore left
with those that at one time formed the majority in this category:
on the one hand, privately-run nurseries providing all-day care
and, on the other, small private nursery schools run for profit.
Because the statistics are now swamped by the growth of playgroups, it has become very difficult to estimate the number of
private nurseries of the traditional kinds, and even harder to say
how many provide little more than day care and how many some

form of nursery education. A few, most certainly, provide nursery education quite comparable with that in maintained schools; the vast majority, probably, do not. Indeed, I can state from personal knowledge, that a private nursery school, if staffed and equipped on the standards obtaining in maintained schools, cannot, if its fees are moderate, pay its proprietor what she would earn as a qualified teacher. A survey quoted by Yudkin (1967) also provides a pointer, showing that in terms of professional qualifications, the staff of private nurseries tend to fall short of those of local-authority day nurseries, let alone those of maintained nursery schools. I propose, therefore, to omit private nurseries (in the sense in which I am using the term) from our estimates of the total provision of nursery education.

(iv) *Playgroups.** The recent expansion of playgroups has been so rapid that an up-to-date picture cannot be given from official statistics which in any case include them with other provision of a rather different kind. On numbers, therefore, I shall rely on the very latest figures given me by the two main organisations sponsoring playgroups: the Save the Children Fund (SCF) and the Pre-school Playgroups Association (PPA). Both bodies aim to provide a form of nursery education rather than simply child care.

The SCF led the way: its first playgroup opened in 1954. The SCF playgroups are concerned exclusively with meeting the needs of city children aged two to four 'whose home conditions—high flats or overcrowded tenements—would otherwise deny them the opportunity for free play . . .' By January 1971 there were 118 SCF playgroups, including 19 in hospitals and the number of children helped was about 5 500.† Leaders of SCF playgroups

---

* For further information about playgroups, see E. Molony, (ed.) *How to Form a Playgroup* (BBC Publications 1967). A great deal of the information to be given in the following pages regarding playgroups associated with the Pre-school Playgroups Association is derived from E. Keeley, *1,020 Playgroups* (PPA 1968). This pamphlet reports very fully on a postal survey conducted by the Association in November 1967, with responses from about a third of the playgroups then linked with the Association. I am also greatly indebted to Mrs Mary Bruce, General Secretary of the PPA, for checking my account and for giving me the latest available information on numbers.

† Information kindly supplied by the SCF.

usually have nursery nursing qualifications and have the advice of supervisors who are qualified nursery teachers. Most s CF playgroups are open ten sessions a week, but the children normally attend part-time. There is a very small charge per session which may be waived in cases of hardship. The expansion of s CF playgroups has been limited by the facts that they pay professional salaries and serve families that can themselves contribute little. So the greater part of the cost has fallen on s CF funds, (on which there have been heavy demands in recent years for work overseas)— though some local authorities have been able to give some help with finance, accommodation, and in other ways.

In contrast, the PPA originated in the voluntary efforts of (mainly) middle-class mothers, impatient at the slow growth of nursery education, to help themselves and each other. Most (though not all) such playgroups are now linked with the Association, founded in 1961, which has given the movement effective leadership and a channel for the exchange of ideas, and provided local playgroups with sound guidance both on organisational and educational problems. The Association's thinking and the practice of the best playgroups are on the lines of nursery education— though there are usually limitations of accommodation and equipment compared with a maintained nursery school or class. Some good courses for playgroup staff have been planned and often provided by the PPA, or run in conjunction with the LEA, colleges of education, or other sources of help.

Most playgroups make use of church halls, community centres, or other premises which they are able to hire for a fairly modest rent (usually less than £1 a session); such 'hall groups' have places, on the average, for some 24 children at a time. A minority of playgroups ('house groups') meet in private houses, normally of one of the mothers, and here the average number of places is about twelve. The number of children on the registers is often considerably more than the number of authorised places, since some two-thirds of the children only attend one or two sessions a week. Most playgroups are open in the mornings only, usually for about 2½ hours, and to be open three mornings a week is typical, though some are open for five. Most of the children are aged three and four, but more than half the groups in 1967 accepted some children under three, though this practice is diminishing. More than half have some children who have turned five. Fees are commonly 15p or 20p per child per session, but can be as low as $7\frac{1}{2}$p if groups are subsidised by grant aid.

In playgroups associated with the PPA, the person in charge of each is called a 'supervisor'. In 1967 about two-thirds of the supervisors of hall playgroups and a third of those of house playgroups had some relevant qualification, for example in teaching (though not always in nursery teaching) or in nursery nursing. The Association estimates that the proportion of unqualified supervisors has probably risen during the period of rapid expansion since the survey. However, a high proportion of supervisors have attended courses devised specially for playgroup staff. The staff usually receive payment of £1 or less per session; many (including a few supervisors) serve without payment; if they are mothers of young children attending the playgroup, their children have free places on the day that they help. The supervisor will usually have at least one regular assistant, or parents may help on a rota basis. In general, parental co-operation is greatly welcomed —as a matter of major principle—both to reduce the child/adult ratio and to give parents a strong sense of involvement in a joint enterprise. A child/adult ratio of 8:1 is recommended and is commonly achieved.

Financially, most playgroups operate on a shoe-string and it is remarkable that this service can work as well as it does on what, in the public sector, would be regarded as a tight budget. This is largely because much of the help is voluntary or, if the staff are paid, the payment is far below that for comparable work in the public sector; moreover equipment is sometimes limited, especially in a new group, often contrived instead of bought, or secondhand. However, some local authorities now give some help to playgroups in the way of initial grants, reduced rents for premises, or by other means; their power to do so has been increased under the Health Service and Public Health Act 1968. More recently, exchequer grants for selected playgroup projects have been made under the Urban Aid Programme. The DES has also helped by making a grant towards the appointment of a National Adviser to the Association, and this grant has now been increased so that an additional adviser can be employed.

According to the latest estimates (September 1970) issued by the Association, its membership covers some 6 000 playgroups catering for over 130 000 children. There are 130 branches, guiding playgroups locally, and some 170 voluntary area organisers. This is a formidable achievement, the outcome of energetic leadership, public-spirited voluntary effort, and a crying need.

Keeley's survey indicated that perhaps 10 per cent of the children in PPA playgroups had already turned five. Making an approximate deduction for these and adding those catered for by the SCF, we reach a total of about 122 000 children aged two to four catered for by the two main playgroup organisations. This is rather more than the number provided with some form of nursery education in grant-aided schools, and this without reckoning those playgroups which have been influenced and guided through the PPA's publications without being linked with it through membership. How far are playgroups to be regarded as providing nursery education?

In reaching an answer, let it first be said that one can fully appreciate the concern of nursery educationists to maintain what may be called *identifiable* standards: indeed, it is this vigilance for quality which has enabled nursery education to give a lead in some respects to other types of primary school. Even so, it obscures the issue to draw hard-and-fast lines and to say 'This is *true* nursery education, that is not', where the criterion used is, for example, whether or not the teacher has had a college of education nursery training. To do this is to seek an easy way out, to substitute a simple administrative criterion for any real thinking about what goes on and what the children gain. Who can say with any confidence that an intelligent mother of young children, perhaps a graduate, who has attended courses and done some reading, can *never* provide nursery education of comparable quality to that offered by some young teachers fresh from college? Obviously, such a generalisation could hardly be sustained by a careful examination, not of paper qualifications, but of what in fact goes on. Indeed, it might well turn out that in some aspects of the work, for example in psychological insight and in fostering intellectual development, the intelligent, mature, well-educated mother might show more subtlety and experience than the girl fresh from college. What I think we have to realise is that both in maintained nursery education and in playgroups we are inevitably dealing with *ranges* of quality, and that the ranges for maintained schools and for playgroups overlap. Almost certainly the range of quality in maintained nursery education averages higher than in playgroups, partly because the teachers are nearly all trained, and partly because equipment and accommodation in the maintained sector are usually better. Still, these overlapping ranges of quality do together form a continuous spectrum in which it is hard to distinguish 'true' nursery education from something which isn't.

In certain respects it can even be said that playgroups have what may count as advantages compared with maintained nursery education. The child/adult ratio is usually more favourable than in the maintained sector. The break from home may be less acute in a small intimate community which may include the child's family friends, and adults who are known to him. Attendance may be only one or two mornings a week instead of being at least half-time as is normal in the maintained sector; and if it is said that this is time lost to education, the answer could be that one or two mornings a week may be about right for many children as their first taste of school, especially if the home is stimulating. Then there is the fact that nearly three-quarters of the playgroups linked with the PPA are not open five mornings a week and few are open any afternoon, so not many mothers can use the playgroup to care for the child when they go out to work, even part-time. For some mothers this may be a disadvantage, but for the children a boon, since they will usually be with their mothers in the mornings that remain, as well as in the afternoons. For many children this could be a very satisfactory pattern for beginning school.

Finally, and all-important, the very foundation of the playgroup movement is the notion of parental involvement in the education of children. It is a family-oriented provision, in which children and parents are educated together into a better understanding of their relationships. Maintained nursery education is moving towards such a conception; for the playgroup, it is an essential part of its very nature.

Pre-school playgroups can no longer be ignored. They aim to provide and often succeed in providing a genuine form of nursery education for rather more children of this age than are catered for in grant-aided schools. It seems likely that, because of the advantages listed above, they should have a continuing share in the ultimate provision, especially for children of three, getting their first experience of social play away from home. We shall come back to this possibility later (pages 85 and 162–3).

Meanwhile, it must be acknowledged that the contribution of playgroups (other than those of the SCF) to nursery education in working-class neighbourhoods is still quite small, though the support given by the Urban Aid Programme will extend this side of the work. Even so, PPA playgroups began as a venture in middle-class self-help and have largely remained so. The small charge would deter some working-class mothers, and a playgroup open only, say, three mornings a week would not help those who seek part-time work. There may also be something in Yudkin's speculation (1967) when he asks 'whether more subtle feelings of class made many working-class women reluctant to join groups which were mainly started by a few middle-class housewives.' The pre-school playgroup movement could play a most valuable part (as it tries to do) in breaking down class barriers—and how could this better be done than through the shared interest of mothers of all classes in their children?

HOW MUCH IN ALL?

Having reviewed all aspects of pre-school provision, it remains to do some adding up. We have already seen that some 104 000 children aged two to four were receiving some form of nursery education in grant-aided schools. That was in January 1969. But by the end of 1971 this number will have been increased by about

16 000 through the implementation of the first two phases of the Urban Aid Programme.[11] So a completely up-to-date figure for grant-aided schools is approximately 120 000. If we add the approximate figure of 30 000 children receiving a form of nursery education in independent schools, we reach a grand total of some 150 000 such children in schools qualifying for inclusion in the *Statistics of Education.*

How many more are receiving a form of nursery education by other means? Here I am myself obliged to draw an arbitrary line in what is in fact a fairly continuous spectrum ranging from good nursery education to minimal child minding. In doing this, I propose to reckon as providing nursery education those agencies which make this their chief *aim*, as distinct from those which seek primarily to provide care. This means that we include playgroups associated with the SCF and the PPA, but exclude day nurseries, child minders and the residential and foster care recorded hitherto by the Home Office. I think too we must exclude what remains of the 'private nursery' category (other than playgroups), since many private nurseries are simply private day nurseries, and others, though claiming to be schools, have very little relationship to nursery education as we know it. Finally, I am omitting playgroups not associated with one of the two main organisations: a fair number exist, but we have no means of assessing their educational aims, and the fact that they have not taken the trouble to identify themselves with a national movement must give us doubts.*

This is a rough-and-ready division. One realises that some of those aiming to provide nursery education may not achieve their aim with much success. On the other hand, some agencies which chiefly claim to provide child care (like the best day nurseries) may in fact provide something more. So our errors may cancel out.

We have seen that the total number of children aged two to four served by playgroups associated with the SCF and PPA is now

---

* As it gains momentum, the Association of Multi-racial Playgroups, which is beginning to promote the formation of voluntary playgroups in immigrant areas, may constitute a third nationally-linked chain of playgroups making a substantial contribution to the total numbers, and this in a field where the need is great.

about 122 000. Adding these to the number, in 1971, in schools included in the *Statistics of Education*, we arrive at a grand total of some 272 000 receiving what *aims* to be education for children of nursery age. This is 10·8 per cent of the child population aged two to four inclusive.

Having arrived at this magical percentage figure—as others have tried to do before me*—what does it tell us? Certainly it does not in itself reveal the percentage of all children who *pass through* some form of nursery education on their way to the infant school. Yet this is a far more significant measure than the global percentage of two-to-fours in school or playgroup—especially as it is generally agreed that school is not the right place for most children of only two.

To arrive at this more significant measure of *nursery experience*, we need to know the age-composition of the 10·8 per cent of the two-to-four age-group who are in nursery education. The fours predominate, and it will be rare for a child to be recorded as in nursery education at three, and for him then to abandon school until he enters the infants. So the percentage of four-year-olds in nursery education should be a good indication of those gaining some form of nursery experience on their way to the infant school. The calculation is not simple,[12] not least because it must exclude rising-fives who have just entered an infant class from home, but include rising-fives who have just been promoted from nursery education.

We arrive at an estimate of approximately 115 000 in grant-aided and independent schools covered by the *Statistics of Education*—though this estimate might well be three or four thousands out either way. It takes account of the expansion up to 1971 under the Urban Aid Programme. In playgroups, we estimated that

* It is not easy to compare my figure with earlier estimates, since they were made before the very recent large expansion of playgroups and since they often include children receiving only care. For example, Howe's estimate for 1964 of 7½ per cent of the two-to-four age-group includes those in day nurseries, private nurseries and with child minders. Plowden (para. 293) gives a figure for 1965, for England only, of 7 per cent 'receiving some form of education in a school or nursery class.' However, this percentage relates to the five years 0–4 inclusive, and Table 4 shows that it comprises children receiving almost *every* kind of education and care, and also 110 527 rising-fives, most of whom had just entered school.

there were about 122 000 children aged two to four, and a reasonable guess, confirmed by the PPA for their playgroups, is that about half of these were four-year-olds. We arrive, therefore at a grand total of some 176 000 children now gaining some form of nursery experience on their way to the infant school. This is 21·0 per cent of the total child population aged four.*

A number of surveys bear out this figure if we take account of recent expansion. For example, the National Survey conducted for Plowden (vol. 2, appendix 3), included 3 092 children aged 7 or 8 or 11 in June 1964, so they became five in 1958, 1961 or 1962. Sixteen per cent of them were said to have attended a nursery school or class, maintained or independent. Bearing in mind that this refers to a period around 1960 before the recent expansion of playgroups had begun, it seems to confirm that a present figure of about 21·0 per cent is not an over-estimate.

The National Survey findings also illustrate the fact that the provision is most unevenly spread. The sixteen per cent found as the average proportion of nursery experience for England as a whole was also broken down into percentages for the ten English divisions of the DES. These divisional percentages ranged from 36 per cent for the Metropolitan division down to 9 per cent for the Eastern division (East Anglia). An even bigger contrast is shown by Howe (1966) who tabulates for various cities the number of places in nursery schools and classes and in day nurseries. Leicester comes out with 112 such places per thousand population under five, and Plymouth with only 11·4.

Nor are the social classes equally served. If the National Survey's average of 16 per cent is broken down in this way, it appears that the children of professional-class parents came off best with 25 per cent getting nursery experience, those of the unskilled came next with 20 per cent, and the intervening social classes at or below the average. This is to be expected, since nursery schools and classes have most often been provided in

* Since the sources of my statistics range over the period 1969 to 1971, I have taken the figure for 1970 (840 000) for the number of four-year-olds in the child population. The percentage figure 21·0 per cent is made up of 11·2 per cent in grant-aided schools, 2·5 per cent in independent schools, and 7·3 per cent in playgroups.

slum areas and since, even in 1960, professional-class neighbourhoods were often well supplied with private nurseries. The
proliferation of playgroups and the Urban Aid Programme,
between them, may intensify this contrast between what is
available, modest though it is, at the extremes of the class structure,
and the paucity of provision for those in the middle.

Such facts as these reveal the extent to which our provision for
the education of young children has been left to chance: the
chance on the one hand of local concern for the under-privileged,
and on the other of local middle-class effort. It must be left to
chance no longer; the time has come to plan.

THE CASE FOR EXPANSION

We turn then to the need for expanding the provision for children
before they enter the infant school. Here, fortunately, the case
has already been made briefly but cogently in Plowden (paras.
296–305) and with eloquent detail by van der Eyken (1967). Here
it is only necessary to state the case in broad outline. We look at it
first in terms of the needs of the children themselves and then in
the broader context of the whole family.

In the early days of nursery education much of the impetus
came from a growing concern about the physical health of the
children of the poor. Margaret McMillan rejoiced at the virtual
disappearance of rickets among the children attending her nursery
school in Deptford, some 80 per cent of whom arrived with signs
of the disease. She herself saw that there was much more to
nursery education than this, and indeed held that its most important outcomes were in social and intellectual development.
Nevertheless, such progress as was made in the provision of
nursery education in those early days owed much to the realisation that the children of the poor were being damaged physically
by poverty and neglect, that much of this damage was irrevocable,
and that we were thereby creating a C3 nation. Things are better
now owing to the welfare state and the general rise in living
standards. Nevertheless, there are still families living in nutri-

tional poverty; far more widespread, there is often a gap in effective oversight of the health of the young child between that provided by the maternity and child welfare services and the school medical service, and not enough is known about the long-term loss in health which may result.

So the health hazards of social neglect of the young child remain important. Nevertheless, in the 'thirties, the emphasis began to shift towards the social and intellectual gains through early education, largely under the influence of the work of Susan Isaacs.* Middle-class mothers began to realise that opportunities for social play and for the sharing and mutual stimulus of a larger group were important to the social development of young children in the small families of that period. So nursery education became desirable to the middle class as well as for the working class—and this at a time when few middle-class married women went to work.

The full realisation of the probable intellectual gains from nursery education is of more recent growth, though the McMillan sisters and Susan Isaacs had both emphasised them. It stems particularly from the recent emphasis on language development and the part which this is believed to play in concept formation and mental growth. Here the emphasis has shifted again towards the needs of the child who is deprived and especially those who are culturally deprived. For example, Bernstein† has analysed the language 'codes' of working-class and middle-class homes and shown how the 'elaborated code' of the average middle-class home makes for a more complex quality of thought than the 'restricted code' of the average working-class home. If this is so, social play under skilled guidance in which children are constantly encouraged to set in order a rich variety of experience through free discussion could have a most potent effect on thinking processes and intellectual potential. For the middle-class child, it could carry further the effective speech and thought habits

* S. Isaacs, *Intellectual Growth in Young Children* (Routledge and Kegan Paul 1931) and *Social Development in Young Children* (Routledge and Kegan Paul 1933).

† B. Bernstein, 'Social Class and Linguistic Development: a Theory of Social Learning,' in HALSEY, A. H., FLOUD, J. and ANDERSON, C. A. *Education, Economy and Society* (New York Free Press 1961).

already beginning to be acquired at home; for the working-class child it could go some way to compensate for cultural deficiencies. In other ways too, the rich and varied activities of a good nursery education could be expected to enhance intellectual power. One thinks, for example, of the gradual setting in order of experience about the properties of materials and things, living and non-living, and finding the words for them; of the acquisition through graded experience of basic number concepts; and of the carefully nurtured growth of creative imagination and expression.

All this has been reinforced by a new understanding of the critical importance of the first few years in the development of intelligence. In a brilliant review of a vast body of work, Bloom* has shown that about 50 per cent of the variation in intelligence found at the age of seventeen is already accounted for by the age of four; and moreover that it is in the first four or five years, when intelligence is developing most rapidly, that the cultural environment can have its maximum effect. He claims to show that in identical twins, which have the same heredity, extreme differences in cultural environment can lead to differences in intelligence quotient amounting to as much as twenty points on the IQ scale. As he says, this could mean the difference between a life in an institution for the feeble-minded and a productive life in society; or, in another part of the range, it could mean the difference between an occupation which is at the semi-skilled or unskilled level and a professional career. Yet a considerable part of this kind of difference will already have been decided by what happens to the child up to the age of four or five. As Bloom puts it, 'A society which places great emphasis on verbal learning and rational problem-solving . . . cannot ignore the enormous consequences of deprivation as it affects the development of general intelligence.' Our intellectual assets—at any level—are precious; through neglect of the early years they are going to waste.

When all this has been said, it must be acknowledged that such evidence as we have on the long-term effects of nursery education on learning ability is somewhat conflicting. A number of these studies are well summarised for the general reader by van der

* B. Bloom, *Stability and Change in Human Characteristics* (Wiley 1964).

Eyken (1967). None of them is altogether satisfactory in providing a controlled comparison between children who have had nursery education and a strictly comparable group of children who have not. For one thing, it is often very difficult to trace and eliminate all the factors of selection which enable one child to have nursery education and another not. Often it will be the child who is the more deprived who gets the chance and, although the head teacher who gives this priority may have been aware at the time of the various kinds of deprivation which controlled her judgement, not all of these may be known and allowed for by the investigator when control groups come to be set up. Secondly, the criteria used in comparing nursery and non-nursery children at a later age may be somewhat crude and limited in scope. Not everything of importance is readily measurable, yet it is the qualities which are easily tested, for example mechanical arithmetic and reading which tend to be used.

Lastly, and perhaps most important, we do not yet—even in nursery education—know all the answers. Nursery educationists have led the way in creating the kind of environment in which children are free to learn. It may well be that freedom is not enough, and that a rather more deliberate structuring of the learning environment and of learning situations will produce more startling results in the development of intelligence. Much of our detailed knowledge of young children's thinking and learning, derived from Piaget and others, is so very recent that, despite much lip service, it has hardly as yet been embodied to any marked degree in what the ordinary nursery teacher does. In such matters we may realise in twenty years' time that we were now at the very beginning. There is a great need for studies of the *application* of what is known about young children's learning, on a scale and with resources comparable with those devoted to Nuffield science and Nuffield mathematics. Some very small beginnings are now being made, but they have yet to bear fruit.* I shall return to this question in chapter 7.

* M. Pines, *Revolution in Learning* (Allen Lane 1969) provides a most readable account of some recent developments, especially in U.S.A., in the education of young children.

Meanwhile, in some directions, the problems of intellectual and social deprivation are increasing, since our modern urban environment does not stand still, and not all the changes take much account of the needs of childhood. An increasing number of young children grow up in high flats where there is nowhere to play within the mother's sight, and many still live in tenement dwellings where they have to be kept quiet lest the neighbours grouse. Even for children living in small one-family houses there are great difficulties in finding safe opportunities for social play. In the past, many working-class children living in such houses played in the street, but modern traffic fills mothers rightly with fear. Even if there is a small back-yard, this often gives access to the street; if, as in some midland towns, there is a common back-yard to several terrace houses, the way to the street cannot be controlled. So once the child is outside the back-door, he is unsupervised. The middle-class alternative of inviting children in is not an easy solution in a small working-class home, and raises problems of selection, of finding the right children of the right age, and of counter-obligations. So, many children spend the years until they enter school playing largely by themselves— interspersed with traipsing round, willy-nilly, with their mothers to the shops.

But the child's immediate needs are not the only ones to be considered; they are intimately bound up with the mental health of the mother and so with that of the whole family. A mother and her young child may be good company for each other up to a point, and both gain from the relationship. Up to a point; for soon the mother may come to think of herself as a 'captive wife', a problem so vividly described in the study by the late Hannah Gavron under that title.* The pattern of a woman's life has changed radically in the course of this century. There is no longer a huge reserve of single women to do the increasing number and variety of jobs for which women are well fitted. Women marry younger and live longer. Family limitation has reduced the effective child-bearing period often to a matter of four or five years, when once it extended throughout a third of a shorter lifetime.

* H. Gavron, *The Captive Wife* (Routledge and Kegan Paul 1966).

The normal pattern is now for a girl to leave school and work until marriage at twenty or twenty-one, to continue working till the first baby comes and then, when the last child starts school, or before if she can make suitable arrangements, to return to work often at first part-time, but later often full-time.

During the time when the children are little she may be very lonely, for the traditional 'street life' of the working-class mother in cities is dying out. This depends on a stable population, a street-level front door, and women neighbours who are not, as now they mostly will be, away at work. If, as so often happens, she is in two or three rooms which are unattractive, inconvenient and limiting, she will come to 'hate the sight of them', day after day, and find little stimulus or opportunity to achieve the minor improvements that the middle-class housewife enjoys; even so, she may not find enough to occupy her in any full and satisfying sense throughout the day. Increasingly she may feel inadequate, that she is contributing little to the family's affairs, especially as young husbands in all classes nowadays tend to take a substantial share in household chores and in looking after the children—as both Gavron and the Newsons* have shown. This is one of the most encouraging facts of modern life and yet for the 'captive wife' it may in some measure diminish her status in her own eyes.

There is no wonder that many young mothers (and not only in the working class) begin to look back with nostalgia at the time before the children came, when they were out in the world, and that they long to get back, at least to part-time work. For many of them, of course, this is also a matter of some financial urgency, perhaps giving them the only chance there is of saving enough to rent better accommodation and furnish it, or even to put money down on a house. For some, living in housing conditions which middle-class people find it hard *really* to imagine, this can be a matter of desperate necessity. And yet, many young mothers are filled with guilt at these feelings. They accept at its face value the glib generalisations of so many social pundits, filtered down by way of the women's magazines, that the right

* J. Newson, and E. Newson, *Infant Care in an Urban Community* (Allen and Unwin 1963) and *Four Years Old in an Urban Community* (Allen and Unwin 1968).

place for a mother of young children is with them, *all the time*. Dr John Bowlby has made us all aware of the dangers of mother deprivation, but the notion has often been taken out of its original context and applied in extended and dogmatic ways which he would never have contemplated.*

Like so many things, this is a matter of degree: the age of the child, the length of separation, the gradualness or otherwise with which everything is done. Every arrangement which involves separation of a young child from its mother requires the most careful thought and preparation and a gradual induction into a new situation—much like that described in the last chapter when a child first starts school. Thus, it will often be best if a young child is at first looked after away from his mother, when this becomes necessary on occasion, in the familiar environment of his own home, and by someone such as a close relative, whom he knows and likes. Despite the fact that the 'extended family' is now less common, by far the most usual way of caring for young children when their mother is at work is still with the help of their grandmother, as Yudkin and Holme's data show. For a while this can often be a good arrangement, especially if the mother is only working part-time. Most people will still feel that for a child of under three to be cared for outside the home, away from his mother, even for half days, is better avoided if possible. Sometimes it simply cannot be avoided; then a sufficiency of good day nurseries may be the best answer, especially if the staff realise that they have some responsibility for education as well as care. Over three for many children, and over four for most, a half-day separation, *properly prepared for*, need cause little anxiety, and can soon bring other gains, best of all if the new experience is in nursery education.

What one is looking towards is the gradual growing up in the family as a whole of a new pattern, in which the child is happily learning, and in which the mother is getting out and seeing new faces, feels herself to be making a fresh contribution to the family's

---

*The matter is put in perspective—together with much else that is relevant to the present theme in S. Yudkin and A. Holme, *Working Mothers and their Children* (Michael Joseph 1963).

fortunes, and acquires renewed mental health in the process, to the benefit of husband, children, and all. In addition, her financial contribution may help to relieve many tensions. Family breakdown is one of the key problems of our time; it could often be avoided if, at a critical time in the family's fortunes, the whole pattern of its life could be given this new look.

The case, therefore, for nursery education as thick on the ground as infant education rests not only on the needs of the children—and society's need for their abilities to be made the most of—but also on the need of families to achieve new and fruitful patterns of co-operation and equality. In the next chapter we shall begin to consider some of the ways in which this might be done.

NOTES

1. *Statistics of Education* 1969, vol. 1, table 43.

2. *Op. cit.*, table 5 for full-time pupils, table 8 for part-time pupils. Nursery and special schools are not included in the primary school figures.

3. It is an odd fact that we do not know at all precisely the number of children in properly authorised nursery classes operating on nursery standards. Table 18 gives 50 891 children as attending nursery classes full-time, and Table 8 states that 22 778 children were attending maintained primary schools part-time. Nearly all of these part-timers would certainly be in nursery classes. So it would seem reasonable to conclude that altogether about 73 000 children were attending *authorised* nursery classes, but it appears that this would be a large over-estimate. I am informed by the DES that, for the purposes of Table 18, a 'nursery class' was taken as *any* class, attached to a primary school, in which 90 per cent or more of the pupils were under five. So the full-time total given would include children in any *infant* classes authorised almost entirely for rising-fives. It is true that not many local authorities are in a position to authorise such classes in January; even so, the number of children involved will be quite large. It

follows that any estimate of the number in properly authorised nursery classes must be very rough. However, the particulars given in Table 18 on size of classes provide a clue, and on this basis I estimate the number of children, full-time and part-time in authorised nursery classes at about 60 000. From 1971 onwards the numbers given in this table will be restricted to children in authorised nursery classes.

4. This estimate is mainly based on a survey of LEAs reported by Miss Beryl McAlhone in *Where*, No. 26, 1966. I am very grateful to Miss McAlhone for lending me the actual questionnaire returns for detailed scrutiny. A number of LEAs, mostly quite small, allow children in one or more term-age-groups to enter infant classes a term or even two terms *before* they become rising-fives. It is possible to calculate the approximate total number of children who, in these authorities, according to these local rules, would be *eligible* to enter early. It amounts to about 8 000 in England and 4 000 in Wales. If we assume (a pure guess) that three-quarters of the 12 000 children eligible take up the option, this gives 9 000 in England and Wales entering infant classes earlier than rising-five as a result of LEA policy. If we then allow (another pure guess) another thousand for the rare children admitted early in other authorities for some compassionate reason, we arrive at a total of 10 000 children admitted to infant classes before rising-five.

5. *Statistics of Education* 1969, vol. 1, table 5 for full-timers and table 8 for part-timers.

6. *Op. cit.*, tables 5 and 8. The actual numbers of children aged two to four, full-time and part-time, were: direct grant nursery —804, direct grant grammar—474, direct grant special—366, 'institution and technical'—3, maintained special—1 227.

7. *Op. cit.*, tables 5 and 8. A few independent schools which are 'recognised as efficient', but which do *not* have more than five children of five or over, appear nevertheless to be included in the *Statistics of Education*.

8. Home Office: *Children in Care in England and Wales, March 1969*. The expression 'aged 2 but not of compulsory school age'

is a little ambiguous, since children who on 31 March were 5:3 all but a day would not yet be of compulsory school age that term.

9 and 10. Department of Health and Social Security, *Annual Report* 1969. Table 36 gives the figures for day nurseries and table 37 those for registrations under the 1948 Act. Both groups of figures refer to England only, not England and Wales, and to 31 December.

11. The first two phases (out of four) of the Urban Aid Programme will add 10 626 nursery places to the present maintained provision. (*Times Educational Supplement*, 4 July, 1969). Some of these places are now available and the second phase should be completed during 1971. If we assume that about half the places are full-time and half part-time, the total number of *children* provided for would be of the order of 16 000. If, as in existing nursery schools and classes, taken together, the proportion of four-year-olds is about two-thirds, then the number of four-year-olds provided for by these two phases of the Programme would approach 11 000.

12. The object of the exercise is to find the total number aged four in nursery education, together with any who had just been promoted from nursery education to infant classes as rising-fives. All tables are from *Statistics of Education, 1969* (DES 1970).

Nursery classes. This number has to be found by deducting the number aged two and three in maintained primary schools (tables 5 and 8) from the total number (note 3) in nursery classes, leaving about 44 000.

Maintained nursery schools 16 835 (tables 5 and 8).

Direct grant and special schools 1 788 (tables 5 and 8).

Children under rising-five in infant classes. We may perhaps assume that all the 10 000 estimated in note (4) are aged four.

Nursery children promoted as rising-fives. There will be a fair number of rising-fives in infant classes in January who were in nursery schools or classes before Christmas. At the time of the January count they are not in nursery education, but they have had nursery experience and they are still four-year-olds so they must be included. The proportion of nursery children who are promoted to infant classes as rising-fives will vary widely, but it may not be unreasonable to assume that about half are so promoted. Adding these (as an unknown) to the total four-year-olds in maintained nursery schools and classes, we arrive at an expression for the total of four-year-olds who are or were in nursery education. If we reckon that the spring-born form 28 per cent of these (page 116), we can then calculate that spring-born rising-fives promoted from nursery education to infant classes in January amount to about 10 000.

Urban Aid Programme additions. We have seen (note 11 above) that the number of four-year-olds provided for by the first two phases of the Urban Aid Programme may be about 11 000.

Independent schools. Tables 5 and 8 give a total aged four of 22 689 but, to allow for those who have just entered as rising-fives, this figure should be rounded down to about the same extent as the overall figure for children aged two to four, giving a number aged four of say 21 000.

| Getting the Pattern Right

NURSERY EXPANSION—TACKED ON OR BUILT IN?

Everybody nowadays agrees with the kind of case for expanded nursery education which I have summarised in the last few pages. Or almost everybody, for there have been at least two dissentient voices. Professor C. H. Dobinson* has argued that the right place for most children under five is with their mothers, that an expansion of nursery education would encourage more mothers of young children to go out to work, and that if this loss (as he sees it) is set against any educational gains, then the high cost of an expanded nursery provision would be unjustified. There might be something in this argument if a wholesale expansion of *full-time* nursery education was now envisaged, but this is no longer the case. Instead, there is now wide agreement that the main expansion should be in half-time nursery education, so that the child spends part of the day in school and part with his mother. Moreover, the high cost of expanding nursery provision is quite considerably offset in some of the 'Plowden-type' schemes we shall presently consider, by economies elsewhere. Professor Dobinson was writing before the appearance of the Plowden Report and it is possible that he would now modify his views.

However, another dissentient voice speaks out from between the covers of the Plowden Report itself, in the form of a Note of Reservation (volume 1, p. 486) by one member of the Plowden Council, Mrs M. Bannister. She agrees with her colleagues that nursery education needs to be expanded in educational priority areas, but elsewhere favours an expansion of 'play centres and play groups', open all day and all the year, and catering for a much wider age-range than nursery education. She envisages that

* C. H. Dobinson, *Schooling 1963–1970* (Harrap 1963).

'mothers should play a full part in helping to run them' and that her proposal, unlike nursery education, would not 'disrupt the mother, child and sibling relationship.'

Quite possibly, there may be a continuing place, in some areas, for voluntary playgroups to provide the very first taste of social play away from home for children who are not yet quite ready even for part-time nursery education. It would have the further merit of initiating the valuable involvement of mothers in their children's education. But most people would hardly agree that such self-help could take the place of an expansion of nursery education run on professional lines and closely integrated with the rest of primary education. This is not an 'either-or' situation; there can be room for both types of provision.

The few dissentient voices can be welcomed, if only to break the monotonous unanimity of support. Such lip service to nursery education has almost given it the status of the prize bore among educational causes—despite the many that could vie for this distinction. To most readers of the educational press, it has become a worthy cause rather than an exciting one. Simply to ask for more of a good thing—full stop—is not a battle-cry that thrills the blood.

Yet, before the Plowden Council began its work, in 1963, much of the advocacy of nursery education was on these lines, just that there should be more of it—tacked on, as it were, to the existing pattern of infant education. The alternative approach was rarely adopted: to look afresh at the nursery and infant stages of education as a whole and see whether a better pattern of early schooling could be devised, so that nursery expansion, when it came, could be built in as part of this better pattern. This is the way we shall try to tackle the problem in this chapter.

WHERE DO WE START?

But first let us remind ourselves of some salient features of the present position, which we reviewed in detail in the last chapter and in chapter 1. In doing so, it may be helpful to summarise the

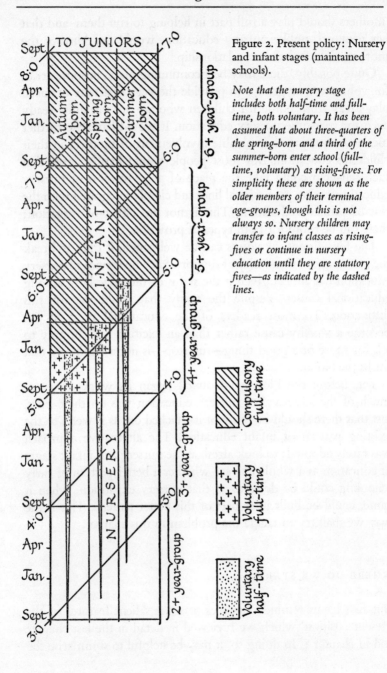

Figure 2. Present policy: Nursery and infant stages (maintained schools).

Note that the nursery stage includes both half-time and full-time, both voluntary. It has been assumed that about three-quarters of the spring-born and a third of the summer-born enter school (full-time, voluntary) as rising-fives. For simplicity these are shown as the older members of their terminal age-groups, though this is not always so. Nursery children may transfer to infant classes as rising-fives or continue in nursery education until they are statutory fives—as indicated by the dashed lines.

present pattern in a flow diagram (figure 2), especially as this type of diagram will also be used in describing the two Plowden proposals and the London Plan, which are less familiar. This diagram (for maintained schools only) concentrates on the nursery and infant stages and can therefore show the sequence in more detail than in figure 1. In figure 2, a slightly different convention has been used. The vertical lines, cutting at right angles across the diagram, mark the beginnings of school years, in September. Where necessary, similar lines indicate the beginnings of the spring and summer terms, in January and April respectively. You will see that there are also diagonal lines, each labelled with an age: 3:0, 4:0, 5:0, and so on. Each diagonal line connects the birthdays of children reaching a given age in the course of a year; for example, the 4:0 line runs from the oldest children in the year-group who became 4:0 on 2 September to the youngest in the year-group who do not become 4:0 till the following 1 September. The square crossed by this diagonal therefore represents the 3+ year-group—those who had reached the age of 3:0 but not the age of 4:0 before the school year began. As we have seen already (page 14–15), they continue to be regarded as 3+ throughout the school year, even though some of them reach the age of 4:0 quite early in the autumn term—crossing the 4:0 diagonal. Finally, we can note that any one of these year-group squares is made up of three oblongs, each containing a term-age-group. The upper one contains the oldest, autumn-born children, born between 2 September and the end of the Christmas holidays. The middle oblong contains the spring-born, with birthdays in the spring term and Easter holidays. The lower oblong contains the summer-born, with birthdays in the summer term and summer holidays. These term-plus-holiday periods differ a little in length—though how much, depends on the date of Easter, and local decisions. Generally speaking, however, the summer period is the longest, the autumn rather less, and the spring period the least, and this is allowed for in the diagram. In terms of *children* the size of the age-groups is also affected slightly by the varying monthly incidence of births.[1]

Having disposed of these technicalities, we can now trace the children through and see what happens to them. Nursery education is represented approximately by the all-too-thin triangles on the left, extending a little beyond the 3:0 line to children who are still only two, but mostly limited to three and four-year-olds, and especially fours. All of it is voluntary, but it may be half-time or full-time as shown. The vast majority of children, however, have their first taste of school in infant classes, full-time, and here the opportunities of the three term-age-groups differ. Virtually all of the autumn-born enter school in September as rising-fives, and then have a full three years of infant schooling before going on to the juniors at rising-eight. Many of the spring-born, perhaps three-quarters[2] on average, enter school as rising-fives in January. If so, they have two years and two terms of infant schooling. The other quarter or so of the spring-born have to wait till after Easter, when they enter as statutory-fives, and then have two years and a term of infant schooling. As to the summer-born, probably only about a third of them get in as rising-fives after Easter,[3] which gives them two years and a term of infant schooling. The remainder have to wait till September when they enter as statutory fives and have only two years in the infants before they transfer to the juniors. They have the further handicap of being the youngest in the year-group and so are often under-estimated. All this can be seen clearly in the diagram. A further point is also apparent: when children enter an infant class as rising-fives they normally do so full-time—the kind of experiment in half-time schooling described on page 46-7 is still quite rare. On the other hand, attendance of rising-fives is voluntary: it is not required by law. Most of them, in fact, do take up the option if it is available, but they need not do so.

This is the present position with its curious anomalies—now, I hope, familiar:

1. Great variation in length of infant schooling—from two years to three years.
2. Considerable variation in age of entry to full-time infant schooling—from 4:8 to 5:4.

These two anomalies depend quite arbitrarily on when the child's birthday happens to come and its relation to local practice and local pressures.

3. A rigid all-or-nothing age of entry to compulsory full-time schooling, or, as Plowden puts it (para. 1236) 'a sudden transition from whole time home to whole time school, from the day with mother to the day with teacher.'
4. Admissions two or three times a year, leading often to great pressure of numbers in the summer term, a 'shuffle-up' of children from class to class in order to make room at the bottom, and instability of staffing.

It is not surprising that the Plowden Council and others who have thought seriously about this problem have racked their brains to find ways of changing this situation. This is one reason why any expansion of nursery education needs to be built into a new pattern of infant schooling, rather than tacked on to the old pattern.

WHAT IS THE RIGHT PATTERN?

But a solution is not easy. To help us in finding it, it may be useful to list some of the criteria against which it can be tested:

1. The expansion of nursery education to meet the needs of all children whose parents wish it should take place as soon as possible. But how soon is 'soon'? The case stated by van der Eyken (1967) or for that matter in Plowden and in Chapter 3 of this book, does not brook delay. Yet even the Plowden Council, writing in 1966, were thinking in terms of the maximum demand not being met completely until the 1980s (para. 1195). This, I submit, is altogether too slow. And yet one must accept that the expansion of nursery education by conventional means—tacked on rather than built in—is a costly process. If the cost were just a matter of money—of cutting down on some less valuable aspect of our affluent society—many would feel that this presented no great problem. But this is not so; it also involves scarce manpower —teachers and nursery assistants—and scarce building resources.

It follows that a *rapid* development of nursery education can only be achieved by means which involve some re-deployment of existing resources for the education of young children, as well as their expansion.

2. For most children, nursery education should be half-time and for nearly all children the pattern for beginning school should be half-time at first, full-time later. The conviction that this is educationally right has been gaining ground ever since the first detailed study of part-time nursery education was made by the LCC Inspectorate in 1956.* Plowden is in no doubt whatever on this point (paras. 317, 353–356).

3. Nursery education needs to be as thick on the ground as infant education, which means that it must normally (though not exclusively) be associated with the primary schools, so that ultimately every primary school containing infants has also some provision for the nursery stage. In short, nursery education should be a *neighbourhood* provision, just round the corner, not something which for mothers and children entails any considerable journey. Most mothers will not want, for the sake of a half-day's schooling for their children, to take them as much as a mile, then return, and two hours later, traipse all the way back again, and return.

4. There should be maximum continuity with the infant stage; in fact, much will be gained if the sharp distinction which at one time grew up between nursery education and infant education is now blurred. We would then be thinking of the education of young children from three to eight as a continuous whole. This would inevitably follow if the greater part of any new nursery provision was in association with neighbourhood primary schools.

5. There should be wide scope for parental choice as to when a child begins school, part-time, or moves on to full-time attendance. Especially before a child begins school at all, his parents know him better than anyone else and are often, though not always, the best judges of whether he is ready.

6. Nevertheless, it is clear that a statutory age for compulsory

---

* This report was published as an LCC Education Committee document in June 1957. It so happens that I was chairman of the working party which undertook this study, and wrote their report.

full-time schooling must be retained; otherwise the children of parents who are shiftless or indifferent or eccentric may suffer through the parents' failure to arrange for them to begin school or to attend regularly having begun. If it is thought that 'part-time before full-time' is the right pattern for nearly all children, there may also be need for a statutory requirement to begin part-time schooling by a certain age, though this is a more controversial point.

7. Despite such statutory requirements, which will be geared to the needs of the vast majority of children, there may still need to be some flexibility in the case of the exceptional child, though under suitable safeguards.

8. For many children, the age of compulsory full-time schooling could, with advantage, be a little later than the law now requires, though not, in my opinion, much later.

9. As far as possible the quite arbitrary effect of date of birth on infant schooling should be eliminated. It leads, as we have just seen, to very wide variation in (i) length of infant schooling, (ii) age of admission to full-time schooling. Both are important.

10. At present, summer-born children suffer from being young within the year-group as well as from having a shorter infant schooling. That they are young cannot be altered, but if admission arrangements can be devised which compensate for this in some degree, that would be an advantage.

11. As far as possible, stability of classes and of staffing throughout the school year should be sought.

12. It is of the greatest importance that any scheme for the expansion of nursery education should not entail any worsening of present nursery standards. For example, the full nursery standard of accommodation, laid down by the Department of Education and Science, is 25 sq.ft per pupil, though this is not always attained, and good nursery work is done in many rooms which fall short. As regards staffing, the standard adopted in nursery classes in most good authorities is a maximum class roll of 30*

---

* In some new rooms provided under the Urban Aid Programme, space on nursery standards is provided for a class of up to forty, but this is to be staffed by two trained nursery assistants in addition to the qualified teacher.

under the guidance of one qualified teacher and one trained nursery assistant, or two nursery assistants in training. It sometimes happens that 'as a temporary measure' the qualified teacher may be replaced by an experienced nursery assistant. In some authorities this may become a chronic situation—in my view a practice greatly to be deplored.

In this matter of standards we must be fair—in two directions. In judging the merits of a scheme it would be wrong to accept standards, whether for children of nursery or infant age, which fall short of those normally applied in the best authorities. On the other hand, we must not condemn a scheme just because it does not, at the same time, achieve some other desirable goal, for example, a reduction in the rolls of infant classes. The comparison must be made with the present situation and these other advances, which we all desire, be made by other means. When this has been said, we should also note that a plan for nursery and infant education will not be very acceptable to the rest of the profession if it can only be achieved by a large transfer of resources from other stages, or if its achievement would entail such a strain on manpower that the steady improvement in staffing that is at last in sight would be brought to a halt.

PROPOSALS TO PLOWDEN

In August 1963, the Central Advisory Council for Education (England) was 'reconstituted', under the chairmanship of Lady Plowden, in order 'to consider primary education in all its aspects and the transition to secondary education.' Its report, issued in January 1967, is commonly known as the 'Plowden Report'.

Almost the first thing that the Council did, in November 1963, was to send out a very detailed questionnaire to a large number of associations representative of local authorities and teachers, to various other associations and institutions concerned directly or indirectly with primary education, and also to a random sample of some 2 500 teachers. Four of the questions had a particular reference to our theme of 'starting school':

1(*a*) How far do you think chronological age is a satisfactory criterion for entry and transfer within and from primary education? How much flexibility should there be at various stages? In particular, how far does lack of flexibility in entry and promotion prejudice the future of children born in the spring and summer?

1(*b*) At what age should nursery or infant education become *available*, and its provision an obligation on the LEA, for children other than those with very exceptional problems?

1(*c*) At what age should education, whether part-time or full-time, be made *compulsory*?

1(*d*) From what age should full-time (morning and afternoon) education be:
(i) available
(ii) compulsory?

These were searching questions and it is worth while to consider briefly the answers given to them in the evidence submitted to the Plowden Council by three important bodies of opinion: the National Union of Teachers (NUT), the Nursery School Association (NSA) and the London County Council (whose education functions were soon to be taken over by the Inner London Education Authority). In thinking about their answers we shall need to bear in mind the criteria discussed in the last few pages.

(i) *National Union of Teachers**

The relevant part of their evidence begins by calling attention to the cultural and linguistic deprivation from which many children suffer; a case for earlier schooling is based mainly on these grounds. The Union is quick to grasp the nettle that in most other advanced countries, compulsory schooling begins at a *later* age than in Britain, commonly at six, sometimes at seven. However, the Union goes on to point out that many of these countries have also extensive provision for some type of voluntary schooling at an earlier age, an option which, in some countries, is taken up by a high proportion of pre-school children.

* *First Things First* (NUT 1964).

The Union goes on to recommend that nursery education should be available to all children whose parents wish it from the age of three, and that full-time infant education should be compulsory from the *beginning* of the school year in which a child reaches the age of five. In this way the birthday variation in length of infant schooling would be eliminated; all would have three years of full-time infant education, from 4+ to 7+. What is not mentioned is that the other birthday variation—in age of entry to full-time schooling—would be accentuated. Children would be expected to start full-time school at any age from just four (if born in August) to virtually five (if born in September). And this difference in educational treatment would stem, not from their needs, but from something quite arbitrary—in which months their birthdays happened to come. To say the least, this is a strangely unsophisticated way of tackling a complex problem: simply to push back the *date* of compulsory full-time attendance to the beginning of the school year and ignore completely the *age* implications. And what of the stress and strain on children starting a full day at just four? The Union pooh-poohs the idea that more than a 'very few children' now find a full day tiring, but their evidence on this point is derived from teachers of infants who are rarely less than rising-five. And as we have seen (page 53) the mothers of children who collapse into exhaustion when they get home may have a different story to tell. In fairness, it should be said that the Union recognises the possibility that the School Medical Officer might, in exceptional cases, recommend that a child's entry should be deferred by a term, or that he should, for a time, have a shorter day, though it is suggested that such 'special arrangements' would only be needed in 'very few' cases. This small token of flexibility in what are otherwise rather rigid proposals is to be welcomed, but clearly it does not go far enough. And it is very surprising that the evidence contains no mention whatever of part-time schooling as a normal step on the way to full-time schooling, despite the considerable and successful experience of part-time nursery education which teachers have gained.

Tested by our criteria, this seems a disappointing and ill-considered section of what is otherwise a valuable body of evidence. There is little indication here of fresh thinking on a difficult and complex question. Moreover, the proposals are not even realistic. They would entail reducing the average age of entry to full-time infant education by about five months and at the same time providing nursery education (part-time or full-time is not stated) from the age of three for all whose parents wish it. In terms of manpower and building resources this is a formidable programme which, even for the most progressive government, would take many years to complete. Generations of young children cannot wait that long. Yet these are far from being the only proposals in the Union's evidence which make heavy demands on manpower and other resources. Some discussion of logistics and priorities is surely an essential part of the advocacy of proposals which are regarded as something more than pie in the sky; in this body of evidence such discussion is largely lacking.

(ii) *The Nursery School Association**

The NSA submitted, as one might have expected, a well-argued case for the expansion of nursery education. The recommendations relevant to admission to school were as follows:

'1. That the value of the education of the young child be accepted wholly, in its own right, and as the essential beginnings of subsequent optimal development and consequently that statutory provision be made for adequate nursery education for all children whose parents wish for it.

2. That such provision be available for children from the age of 3 years, part-time or full-time, according to the needs of the child. Provision should always be adequate to permit flexibility of procedure to deal with individual variations.

3. That there should be no change in the compulsory commencement school age, but there be permission for some five-year-olds to attend part-time only, until they are adjusted to school life.

* I am indebted to the Secretary of the NSA for letting me see a copy of the Memorandum of Evidence, and also a summary of the replies of 33 branches to the Plowden questionnaire, and a subsequent memorandum containing the results of a survey.

4. That, because of the adverse effect on children born in the fourth quarter* of the school year:

    (a) It be possible for children who attain the age of 5 during the school year to be admitted to school during the first term, to a reception class organised according to nursery school standards.

    (b) If children are already receiving education in a nursery school or nursery class, they should remain there until the beginning of the term following their fifth birthday.'

With regard to the statutory age, it will be seen that the Association recommended no change, but with flexibility in two directions:

    (a) Some five-year-olds would be allowed to attend only part-time until 'adjusted to school life'. (Any limit?)

    (b) Provision for voluntary attendance from September of children becoming five during a school year, but on nursery standards. In effect this last provision is already covered by the more general recommendation of nursery education for all who wish it.

It will be seen that the NSA proposals are far more flexible than those of the NUT. They would still require a fairly large increase in staff and accommodation compared with the present situation. If they are still pie in the sky, they are a little nearer to earth.

There are certain other points in the NSA evidence of some interest. It appears that the branches consulted were equally divided on the age of compulsory full-time attendance: half favoured five years and half six. However 'the difference of opinion is less than it appears . . . Those who favoured 5 years wanted permission for some children *not* to attend if it were considered undesirable; those who favoured six years wanted sufficient provision for all children who were ready for part-time and more

---

* The reference is to the summer-born, but to describe these as 'children born in the fourth quarter of the school year' seriously understates the problem, since the summer-born have birthdays extending over about 4½ months and comprise 39 per cent of each year-group (see page 116).

especially full-time education *before* the statutory age.' The vast majority of branches stressed the importance of flexibility to meet individual needs. The NSA evidence favours nursery classes or nursery wings associated with primary schools in preference, as a rule, to the separate nursery school; it does so partly in the interests of continuity, both for the children and in home/school relationships, but also because the cost of separate nursery provision is greater.

(iii) *London County Council*

The Evidence of the LCC to the Plowden Council is a substantial printed book of some 100 000 words, embodying the results of a good deal of research as well as much discussion between administrators, inspectors and teachers. A fair amount of the material was new, the result of surveys or other studies specially undertaken.

The LCC's evidence included proposals in the field of admissions policy, which fall into two parts, long-term and short-term. The long-term recommendation was that schooling should continue to be compulsory from the beginning of the term after the fifth birthday, but that schooling should also be available on a voluntary basis from the September after a child became four, 'normally part-time, but full-time where social and economic circumstances make it desirable.'

However, the Council also put forward short-term proposals applicable 'for a number of years' 'in the present circumstances of teacher supply'. They were based, with some modification, on a scheme prepared by a working party of the LCC Inspectorate. These short-term proposals may be summed up as follows:

1. Full-time schooling would be compulsory for all children from the September after they reached the age of five and, for autumn-born children, also during the summer term preceding that September.
2. An authority would be required to provide half-time schooling for all children from the September after they reached the age of four, if their parents desired it, but this

half-time schooling would be compulsory for autumn-born children in January of that year, and for spring-born children after Easter.

3. Thus, except in the case of the summer-born, half-time education would be compulsory during the term before compulsory full-time schooling.

It was pointed out that another way of stating the statutory requirement under the scheme would be to say that the age of compulsory schooling would continue to be the beginning of the term following a child's fifth birthday but that, except in the case of summer-born children, the first term of compulsory schooling would be half-time.

An investigation of the logistics of the scheme showed that it was surprisingly economical of teachers and accommodation. However, the real significance of this short-term proposal by the LCC is that it was the first published example of what may be called a 'Plowden-type' admission proposal—the first of a series which includes also the two plans of the Plowden Report and the recently-devised *London Plan*. These various plans for the education of young children differ in detail, but they all have five main characteristics:

1. They aim to diminish the influence of date of birth on the pattern of primary education available to a child.
2. They increase the opportunities for parental choice in regard to age of admission.
3. Full-time schooling is preceded by a period, voluntary or compulsory, of half-time schooling.
4. The statutory age of compulsory full-time schooling is raised in some degree for some or all children.
5. The resulting saving in staff and accommodation can then be used to facilitate the extension of school experience, especially half-time, to *below* the present statutory age.

As we shall see in the next chapter, the *London Plan* has a good deal in common with this proposal in the LCC evidence to Plowden. However, those of us who devised this proposal, as we now look back on it in the light of Plowden, can see that it has some defects. In particular, there is less flexibility to meet the needs of the exceptional child than we would now like to see. And although our study of the logistics suggested that there would be room for some children of 3+ to attend half-time, the proposal did not aim to provide at all extensively for children of this age. The desire to be 'realistic' in demands for staff and accommodation perhaps weighed with us too heavily, when it would have been better to have had the courage of our convictions and asked for more, even though this might have taken a little longer to realise. Even so, we had produced a first example of a 'Plowden-type' admission proposal, from which there was something to be learnt in devising the more recent *London Plan*.

PROPOSALS FROM PLOWDEN

And so we come to the Plowden proposals themselves, put forward after their three-year labour mainly in Chapters 9 and 10 of the Report. They fall into three categories:

1. *The Nursery Proposals.* Because of their demands on manpower, especially nursery assistants, it was thought that these could not be achieved completely till the 1980s, though much of the expansion would take place earlier.

2. *The Long-term Plan.* This proposal included a radical change in admission age and was linked with the change from infant/junior to first school/middle school transition at 8+. It was emphasised (para. 387) that the *Long-term Plan* should only be implemented when the nursery proposals were approaching full realisation, towards 1980. For this reason Plowden also offered:

3. *The Interim Plan.* This could begin to be operated almost at once, going some way to remedy the worst deficiencies in present admissions policy until the time came when the nursery proposals and the *Long-term Plan* could be fully achieved.

In this account I shall first examine the nursery proposals, then relate them to the *Long-term Plan* with which they are interdependent, and then consider the Interim Plan as a half-way house.

The Plowden Nursery Proposals*

The Report states very clearly that 'part-time attendance should be the normal pattern of nursery education.' (para. 317). 'Our evidence is . . . that it is generally undesirable, except to prevent a greater evil, to separate mother and child for a whole day in the nursery.' (para. 330). The Report goes on to state that 'some mothers who are not obliged to work may work full-time, regardless of their children's welfare. It is no business of the education service to encourage these mothers to do so.' Starting from these beliefs, the Council tries to arrive at a percentage figure for children of 3+ and 4+ who *need* full-time nursery education, and settles for 15 per cent, reached in the following way:

i. On the basis of various studies it is concluded that at least 5 per cent of mothers of children between 3 and 5 work full-time. However a fair number of these children are looked after by grandparents or other relatives, so the proportion in this category in need of full-time nursery education is less than 5 per cent.

ii. 'as many as 10 per cent of mothers have been identified as unable to care effectively for their children. Most of their children ought to receive full-time nursery education.'

iii. 'an unidentified number of children ought to attend full-time because home circumstances are poor. The children of very large families, those from overcrowded homes, homes with only one parent or with sick mothers will have claims on full-time places.'

No doubt Plowden had in mind that there would be some overlapping between these three categories, when it derived from them its 'rough estimate' of 15 per cent. Elsewhere (para. 331) this is

* At this point a matter of terminology needs clarification—as indeed the Report gives it in a footnote to p. 126. When the Report refers to 'three-year-olds' it means children who are 3+ in September, with ages which *then* range from 3:0 to almost 4:0, though some will be four quite early in the autumn term. Similarly with 'four-year-olds'. Sometimes the 3+ children are spoken of as '3s–4s', since some so soon become fours, and the 4+ children as '4s–5s'. It seems a pity so confusing and variable a terminology was used, when the precise terms 3+ and 4+ were available and are sometimes used as well. But one can well understand the desire to escape from time to time from technical terms.

referred to as the maximum demand for full-time nursery education.

A similar attempt is made to estimate the maximum demand for half-time places. It is thought that not more than half the children of 3+ will attend nursery groups, either full-time or half-time, because many parents will consider this too young. So if 15 per cent of the 3+ year-group attend full-time, this leaves 35 per cent half-time. It is also thought that a maximum of 90 per cent aged 4+ will attend nurseries, since 'some parents will be unwilling to allow them to attend nursery groups, others will continue to make private arrangements, and others, particularly in the country, will find the nearest nursery group inaccessible.' Again, deducting the 15 per cent who are full-time, we are left with 75 per cent of the 4+ year-group requiring half-time places. To summarise, Plowden's 'rough estimates' of maximum demand for nursery places (which I shall refer to in future as the 'Plowden percentages') are as follows:

	Half-time	*Full-time*	*Total*
3+	35%	15%	50%
4+	75%	15%	90%

It seems likely that the 35 per cent of the 3+ year-group attending half-time would not be spread evenly over the three term-age-groups; there would tend to be a greater demand from the older, autumn-born children to attend from September than there would be from the summer-born who would then be only just three. At a guess, the average of 35 per cent might be made up of 55 per cent autumn-born, 35 per cent spring-born and 15 per cent summer-born.* These Plowden percentages, so interpreted, are very roughly represented in the nursery part of figure 3 (page 105) which shows the Plowden *Long-term Plan*—but more of this later.

At present, nursery schools (though not, as a rule, nursery classes) accept some children of only two years, and both nursery schools and classes have fair numbers of children not much over

---

* If, in strict accuracy, the differences in size of the three term-age-groups are taken into account, the suggested percentages combine to give an average of 34 per cent, not 35 per cent. But this is near enough for our purposes.

three years. Plowden took the view—quite rightly—that 'most children are too young at two to tolerate separation from their mothers. Some will be ready at three, but for others four will be a better age to join a nursery group . . . Nursery education should be available to children *at any time after the beginning of the school year after they reach the age of three.*' (para. 316, my italics). In other words, local authorities would not be expected to provide for children under 3+, which means, in the case of the autumn-born, not under rising-four. This is a departure from present practice, and is indicated in figure 3, by the sharp cut-off at the September 3+ line. However, it is probably safe to assume that Plowden would not *rigidly* exclude any possibility of earlier admission of children in special need, if room could be found, and I have indicated this assumption in the narrow triangles on the left, extending even, in a few cases, to just before the 3:0 line. As a general rule, however, Plowden took the view that, where it was unavoidable for a child under 3+ to be separated from its mother during the day, it would be better for this provision to be made in day nurseries, and, with the expansion of nursery education for children of 3+ and 4+, the day nursery would be able to cater more extensively for younger children needing this care. It is, however, suggested by Plowden (para. 315) that if some nursery schools shared sites with day nurseries, the latter could take over the care of some of the older children, who needed to be looked after beyond normal school hours.

The term 'nursery group' is introduced (para. 311) for a unit of twenty nursery places which, in the case of part-time attendance, could mean forty children, half in the morning, half in the afternoon. 'Two or three groups might make a unit—to be called a "nursery centre"; or they might be combined with day nurseries or clinics in "children's centres"'. Some separate nursery provision linked with day nurseries, clinics, factories and large blocks of flats is certainly to be welcomed; but it is a little disturbing to find (para. 1193) that only 50 per cent of the new nursery provision is envisaged as associated with primary schools. The case for such association has been argued earlier on page 90, and is also supported by the NSA evidence to Plowden.

Apart from this last point, on which one could wish for a different emphasis, the proposals so far seem admirable. On the staffing proposals, however, there are bound to be misgivings. The Report begins by saying that 'the ideal pattern' would be for each group of twenty children to be in the care of one qualified teacher and one nursery assistant with NNEB or other recognised training. It is said that shortage of teachers would make this out of the question for 'some decades'. Instead, it is proposed that each group of twenty places should be under the day-to-day control of two nursery assistants, who would work under the supervision of a qualified teacher at the rate of one qualified teacher to every sixty places. Where there was a nursery centre of three groups, there would be a qualified teacher in charge who would divide her time between the three nursery groups on the site. On the other hand it also appears that where the provision was in the form of single nursery groups of twenty children, the qualified teacher would be expected to supervise up to three such groups, presumably on different sites. In small schools with small classes, it is suggested that the supervision might be by the head teacher or by an assistant teacher—the latter, no doubt with a small infant class of her own.

Plowden's courageous advocacy of nursery education for all—at a time when quite minor expansion seemed remote—fills one with admiration, and it must have been with considerable misgivings that members accepted the staffing pattern just described. One implication has been very largely overlooked. It is that 'one teacher to 60 *places*' will often mean 'one teacher to 120 *children*', since attendance will usually be half-time. And this could mean 120 children spread over three sites. Great claims are sometimes made for the potential influence of nursery education on intellectual and social growth—indeed, I have made some myself on pages 74 to 76, and return to the point in chapter 7. One hears about the profound understanding of child development which the nursery teacher needs, of the knowledge and insight that she must bring to bear in leisurely conversation with children, so that they acquire through language the power of thought; and of the careful study of each child's social development so that it may be guided aright. Much of this, at its best, entails highly-skilled one-to-one relationships, which cannot be delegated to nursery assistants, whose training, at least in the cognitive aspects of child development, must be limited in depth. It is difficult to conceive that work of real quality can be achieved where the knowledge and gifts of one real professional are spread so thinly. Nor must one forget the understanding and mutual consultation that a good nursery teacher is expected to give to mothers; with 120 to know, she will do well if she only gets to know their names.

No doubt the decision to settle for groups of twenty (instead of the thirty usual in a nursery class) and for one nursery assistant to ten places (instead of the usual one to thirty) was with a view to mitigating the situation just described. But this decision, while reducing the demand for teachers, presented a formidable requirement in rooms and nursery assistants. Groups of twenty mean 50 per cent more rooms than groups of thirty (though they need not be quite so big.) As to nursery assistants, the number required is given (table 37) as 71 700 in 1979, growing to some 85 000 by the date in the 1980s, when full provision for the Plowden percentages was complete. This is a formidable total, not merely to recruit but to train. Moreover, it was decided to give priority to the recruitment and training of teachers' aides, who would come from the same pool of ability as nursery assistants. It is not surprising that the main expansion of nursery education was seen as coming (except in educational priority areas) mostly in the later seventies, and not completed until the 1980s.

The Plowden Long-term Plan

The plan, together with the nursery proposals, is illustrated in figure 3, since the two are inter-dependent. It has the following main characteristics:

    i. The infant school would be transformed into what Plowden calls the *first school*, providing for all children, whatever their birthdays, a three-year course, extending from 5+ up to 8+, when they would transfer to a *middle school* if this was a separate department.

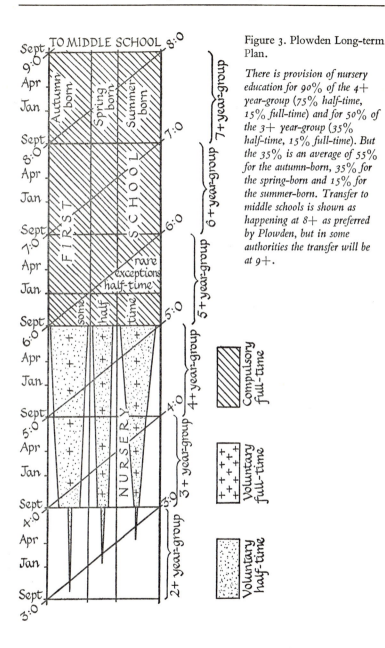

Figure 3. Plowden Long-term Plan.

There is provision of nursery education for 90% of the 4+ year-group (75% half-time, 15% full-time) and for 50% of the 3+ year-group (35% half-time, 15% full-time). But the 35% is an average of 55% for the autumn-born, 35% for the spring-born and 15% for the summer-born. Transfer to middle schools is shown as happening at 8+ as preferred by Plowden, but in some authorities the transfer will be at 9+.

   ii. Full-time schooling would be compulsory for all children (but see iv below) from the September after they reached the age of five, i.e. the average age for starting full-time school (for children not in full-time nursery education) would be 5:6.

   iii. It follows that there would be a *single date of entry* to full-time schooling—September.

   iv. However, there would be some flexibility in the application of this statutory requirement, in that some children would be permitted to attend only half-time in the first term of compulsory schooling, and exceptionally up to the age of six.

   v. The above proposals would only be implemented as nursery education, full-time or part-time, became available to all children whose parents wished it, for at least a year before the age of compulsory full-time schooling, and ultimately for the full Plowden percentages of 3+ children also.

The implications of the plan, when in full operation, for children in the three term-age-groups, are given below. It has been assumed that the full percentage of children of an age-group, expected to attend voluntarily, will in fact attend from September, though in practice some may start later in the year. The exceptional half-time attendance of some children in the first term of compulsory schooling has not been allowed for.

Autumn-born
Voluntary half-time (55%) or full-time (15%) at 3:8—4:0 in September.
Voluntary half-time (75%) or full-time (15%) at 4:8—5:0 in September.
Compulsory full-time in September at 5:8—6:0.
   Average age of entry to school = 4:4; to full-time = 5:6⅓.
Spring-born
Voluntary half-time (35%) or full-time (15%) at 3:4—3:8 in September.
Voluntary half-time (75%) or full-time (15%) at 4:4—4:8 in

September.
Compulsory full-time in September at 5:4—5:8.
Average age of entry to school = 4:1; to full-time = 5:2½.
Summer-born
Voluntary half-time (15%) or full-time (15%) at 3:0—3:4 in September.
Voluntary half-time (75%) or full-time (15%) at 4:0—4:4 in September.
Compulsory full-time in September at 5:0—5:4.
Average age of entry to school = 4:0; to full-time = 4:10⅓.
Overall, the weighted average age of entry is just over 4:1½, and to full-time schooling 5:2.

The plan is clearly a notable advance on present admission arrangements. If the reader will look back to the twelve criteria, set out on pages 89–92, for assessing the merits of proposals he will see that the *Long-term Plan* scores quite well on many of these. In what follows, I refer to these criteria by number.

To begin with, (2) is well satisfied: all children (except for the 15 per cent who begin nursery education full-time) follow the ideal pattern of half-time schooling preceding full-time schooling. Parental choice (5) as to when a child begins part-time school is fully safeguarded. Indeed, Plowden suggests (para. 328) that some of the younger children might attend fewer than five sessions a week and not stay for a whole session, so that entry to nursery education would be very gradual. There is also some flexibility in the age of compulsory full-time schooling (7), in that permission may be granted for the first term of compulsory schooling to be half-time, 'and exceptionally up to the age of six'.* With these exceptions the length of full-time education in the first school is standardised at three years, from 5+ to 8+, thus meeting *one* of the anomalies mentioned under (9). There is some slight compensation to summer-born children for being young within their year-group (10), in that they enter school and start

---

* In point of fact, if the first *term* may be half-time, this would take some of the autumn-born virtually to 6:4 before they were *required* to be in school full-time, but it is not clear whether this was really intended.

full-time attendance a little younger than the others. Finally, there is great stability of staffing through the year (11)—if we assume that most of the children in the percentages indicated do enter in September. In so far as they do not, this could give a more favourable staffing ratio in the earlier part of the year.

But on some criteria, the Plan does less well. Expanded nursery education is only to a moderate extent (50 per cent) linked with the primary schools, and this seems a backward step (3 and 4). In (6) I suggested that if part-time before full-time is the ideal pattern, there might need to be some element of compulsion in support of this, but this is not included. While a *slight* deferment in the age of compulsory full-time schooling may be a positive educational gain (8), it may be thought that an age of 5:8 to 6:0 in the case of the autumn-born is a little late. The birthday handicap (9) is partly met, in that the single date of entry to full-time schooling ensures that all children have three years full-time in the first school. On the other hand, this leads to an even greater discrepancy in *age* of entry to full-time schooling than exists at present, since children may be anything from 5:0 to 6:0 when this time comes, and this is determined quite arbitrarily by the date of a child's birthday. The Report seems to set great store by 'the single date of entry', but the fact that it has also this unfortunate consequence is nowhere made clear. Finally, there is criterion (12)—the maintenance of existing nursery standards. The defects of the nursery proposals in this respect have already been discussed (page 103-4).

I have left aside criterion (1), i.e. the question of the logistics of the *Long-term Plan*—its requirements in manpower and accommodation—and the time-scale which depends on the realisation of these requirements. Plowden approached these questions in a global way, starting from national statistics of the numbers of children in various age-groups, the numbers of teachers and rooms released by the deferment of full-time schooling, and so on. They concluded (para. 334 and table 38) that the expansion of nursery education envisaged 'need not create demands for more teachers'. On the other hand it was accepted that their proposals would entail a large net increase in accommodation, amounting even in

1979 to about 400 000 places (para. 1193), which would mean nearly half a million when the provision was complete. On present accommodation for children at the nursery and infant stages, this is an increase of over 20 per cent. The Plowden estimate of the vast numbers of nursery assistants required has already been mentioned.

My own assessment of the logistics was done in a different way, but with similar results. In the case of the *Long-term Plan*, as with the LCC proposals, I took a series of ideal schools with intakes ranging from 20 up to 120 children in steps of 20, and worked out the number of groups that would be required to meet the principles of the plan. The staffing and accommodation required could then be compared with the staffing and accommodation which would be allowed to these schools under present admission arrangements. The number of teachers required for the 3+ to 6+ year-groups, inclusive, was only about 2 per cent in excess of the number of infant teachers required under present arrangements. If the proportion of nursery teachers now employed in London was also included in the comparison, then the plan actually yielded a small saving in teaching staff. These findings were despite the fact that in the smaller schools it was not always practicable or necessary to give a teacher the oversight of three nursery groups as envisaged in the plan—some had only two. Indeed, it seems as if, in London at least, it would be possible to reduce the number of instances in which a teacher supervised three groups still further and still avoid an increase in teaching staff over those now required. If so, the reduction in quality of teaching would be less widespread than I feared above.

As to accommodation, my findings, by this quite different method, were very similar to Plowden's. The plan required about 30 per cent more rooms for children of 3+ to 6+ inclusive, than present arrangements would require for infants only. If the London proportion of nursery accommodation was also taken into account, the excess required was reduced to about 20 per cent— the approximate figure we reached from Plowden's estimates.

To sum up: the *Plowden Long-term Plan* has many educational merits, but also some educational defects which need to be remedied before it can be accepted as the future pattern. It is economical of teaching staff—but as a result of spreading them more thinly than is educationally desirable. In accommodation it is costly—the result of adopting groups of 20 instead of the present 30. In nursery assistants it is very costly indeed. It was this last factor, more than any other, which limited the rate of nursery expansion under the plan to an extent which none of us— including the Plowden Council—would desire. We shall see that it is possible to devise an alternative which will not only meet the educational defects, but also make for better progress.

The Plowden Interim Plan

Plowden, rightly, linked its proposals on age of starting school with progress towards nursery education for all, in which the recruitment and training of nursery assistants would be the limiting factor. Sufficient progress, it was thought, could not be made before 1977, at the earliest, to justify introducing the *Long-term Plan* before then. However, Plowden was anxious in the meantime to make some progress towards reducing birthday handicaps and also towards achieving the principle of full-time schooling being preceded for most children by part-time schooling. The Report therefore suggests an *Interim* or *Emergency Plan* which could be applied at any time after the necessary legislation had been passed, probably earlier by some authorities than others. This plan is illustrated in figure 4 opposite. There would have been some progress in the expansion of nursery education by the time the *Interim Plan* came into operation and this is indicated in the slightly fatter nursery triangles in the diagram. As will be seen from the right-hand end of the diagram, the change from infant/junior transfer at 7+ to first-school/middle-school transfer at 8+ is not part of this plan, though authorities which found it possible to make this change also at this stage would be allowed to do so.

The plan is as follows:

    i. Children reaching the age of five between February and August would begin full-time attendance the following

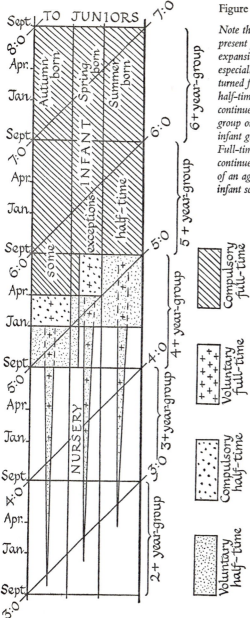

Figure 4. Plowden Interim Plan.

Note that, as compared with present policy, there has been some expansion of nursery education, especially for children who have turned four. It is assumed that half-time nursery children may continue for a while in a nursery group or transfer to a half-time infant group if of an age to do so. Full-time nursery children must continue to be offered full-time till of an age for compulsory full-time infant schooling.

September at a median age of about 5:3. Those reaching age five between September and January would begin full-time attendance after Easter at a median age of about 5:5.

ii. An authority would be required to make half-time education available to all children whose parents wished it, for two terms before full-time entry.

iii. But half-time schooling would be compulsory in the term after a child reached the age of five (if not entitled, that term, by date of birth, to full-time schooling).*

iv. As in the *Long-term Plan*, there is provision for exceptional children to be given permission to attend only half-time during the first term of what would normally be full-time schooling, and very exceptionally up to the age of six.

v. Half-time classes would be kept to half the normal size of infant classes, i.e. on present standards to a maximum of 20.

The implications of the plan for the three term-age-groups (complicated a little by the special situation of the January-born) are as follows:

Autumn-born
Voluntary half-time at 4:8—5:0 in September.
Compulsory half-time in January at 5:0—5:4.
Compulsory full-time after Easter at 5:4—5:8.
Spring-born
   (i) *January-born*
      Voluntary half-time at 4:7—4:8 in September.
      Compulsory full-time after Easter at 5:3—5:4.
   (ii) *February—Easter-born*
      Voluntary half-time at 4:8—4:11 in January.
      Compulsory half-time after Easter at 5:0—5:3.
      Compulsory full-time in September at 5:4—5:7.
Summer-born
Voluntary half-time at 4:4—4:8 in January.
Compulsory full-time in September at 5:0—5:4.

* The exceptions intended in the passage enclosed in brackets are January-born children. They, like the autumn-born, are compulsorily full-time after Easter.

If the option of voluntary half-time schooling were taken up 100 per cent, there would be virtually no room in the half-time classes necessary for the requirements of the plan, to admit any younger children. However, it has been assumed that there would also have been some small expansion of nursery education, supported by other resources than those re-deployed under the plan. The age of entry to compulsory full-time schooling, as compared with the present situation, would be for the autumn-born deferred for a term, for the January-born it would remain unchanged, for the February-Easter-born it would be deferred for a term, and for the summer-born remain unchanged. In practice, however, the deferment for many children would be greater than this suggests, since many are now admitted as rising-fives. But the degree of deferment of full-time schooling is considerably less than in the *Plowden Long-term Plan*, with the consequence that the teachers and rooms made available for re-deployment to cover the half-time admission of younger children are considerably fewer.

How does this plan fare in relation to my criteria set out on pages 89–92? Admittedly it makes little contribution in itself to the expansion of nursery education (1), though it would be accompanied by some expansion met from other resources. It meets the requirement of half-time before full-time (2) very satisfactorily and the half-time classes are closely linked with the primary schools rather than with separate nursery centres (3) (4). There is good provision for parental choice on age of entry (5), yet with some degree of compulsion applied even to part-time entry (6), but there is some flexibility to allow for the exceptional child (7). The age of compulsory full-time schooling is raised, as we have seen, to a moderate degree (8), preferable, perhaps, to that which applies, especially to the autumn-born, under the *Long-term Plan*. The birthday handicap is reduced in both respects: extreme variations both in length of full-time infant schooling and in age of entry to it are avoided—as the second is not on the *Long-term Plan* (9). For the summer-born there is some compensation for being young within the year-group (10), in that they are able to enter both half-time and full-time schooling rather younger than the rest.

I have examined the logistics of the plan by the same methods as were described earlier. One thing that comes out is that the plan entails a very big increase in the teaching staff required as the year goes on. As compared with the autumn term, the spring term seems to require 20 per cent more staff, and the summer 25 per cent. So staffing would be far less stable (11) throughout the year than on the *Long-term Plan*. However, it is suggested (para. 403) that teachers who, in the autumn term, would have a class for only one session in the day, could help in other ways during the other session. In this respect, and some others, the plan comes out very well on educational standards: half-time classes have half the normal roll and are in the hands of a qualified teacher, instead of being under the day-to-day control of a nursery assistant. This is a much more satisfactory arrangement than in the *Long-term Plan*; indeed, in reducing class rolls by half, the plan could even be thought rather generous of qualified staff. On this basis, however, Plowden claims (para. 402) that 'no more teachers will be needed than at present'. My own calculations suggest that (taking the average through the year) the number of teachers required might be raised by about 7 per cent compared with present infant staffing, and that the maximum (summer) accommodation requirements might be raised by about the same proportion. If the maximum size of half-time classes was increased to 35, the staff needed would be about the same as present infant staffing and accommodation a mere 3 per cent up. Moreover there would then be room to admit to half-time schooling some children at a rather earlier age than that envisaged in the plan.

When we look back at this review of its merits, we see that, on quite a number of our criteria, the *Interim Plan* actually scores rather better than the *Long-term Plan*. Why then was it not accepted as the ultimate proposal? One possible reason is that the *Interim Plan* was produced as an afterthought and a stop-gap, when it was realised that the *Long-term Plan* would indeed take a very long time to come to pass. Meanwhile the Plowden Council and its advisors may have become very strongly committed to the idea of a 'single date of entry' to full-time schooling—which is a main feature of the *Long-term Plan*—notwithstanding that this idea has grave defects to offset its merits. Bearing in mind the great pressure under which the Report was completed, and the elaborate logistical calculations already undertaken, it is understandable that the Council did not then begin to think again about its main admission proposal.

However that may be, there is another reason for treating the *Interim Plan* as no more than that: it contributes very little, by way of re-deployment of staff and accommodation, to the expansion of nursery education. For this reason it would take even longer, by this route alone, to achieve nursery education for all—unless very great additional resources could be found.

AN ANSWER STILL TO COME

This chapter has been a long search for a pattern for the education of young children which will be practicable within a reasonable time and educationally right. We began with the setting up of criteria by which we can know the right pattern when we find it. Then followed what, I fear, has been a very laborious review of first one solution, then another; each has been tested and each, in some respects, found wanting.

I hope it will be felt that the labour has been worth while for two reasons. In the first place, it is the two Plowden proposals that now hold the field. They are a great advance on what has gone before. If they are implemented at last, it will be without minor changes, and there will be plenty of problems in putting them into practice. For both purposes, this close analysis from an independent angle may contribute something.

But the Plowden proposals may not be the last word. In looking afresh at them, and at the others we have considered, we may have discovered on our way, parts of one and parts of another which, if combined, could bring us nearer to the right answer we are seeking. This in fact is how the proposals to be discussed in the next chapter came into being.

NOTES

1. If, on average, the spring term begins about 8 January and the summer term about 15 April, then the lengths of the three periods will be roughly: autumn—$4\frac{1}{4}$ months, spring—$3\frac{1}{4}$ months, and summer $4\frac{1}{2}$ months. However, the average daily number of births varies a little from month to month, the highest incidence being in spring and summer and the lowest in October, November and December: *Statistical Review of England and Wales*, 1967 ((Registrar General 1969) Part II, Table T.T.(b)). If this variation is taken into account (averaging the four years 1964–7) it is found that the number of *children* in the three term-age-groups, as percentages of a year-group, are approximately: autumn-born—33 per cent, spring-born—28 per cent, and summer-born—39 per cent.

2. *Statistics of Education* 1969 (HMSO 1970) Vol. 1, p. xvii, gives the number of spring rising-fives in maintained primary schools (other than nursery and special schools), in January 1969, as 17·64 per cent of the whole year-group aged four in the child population. However, this figure refers, in fact, only to children born 1 January to 1 April, so needs to be corrected to cover $3\frac{1}{4}$ months of births. It must also be adjusted to allow for the fact that only about 94·1 per cent of the child population of primary age are in maintained primary schools. With these corrections, we find that about 20·1 per cent of the four-year-olds expected to enter maintained primary schools come in as rising-fives in January. Since, as we have just seen, the spring-born form some 28 per cent of the year-group, we can calculate that in 1969 about 72 per cent of the spring-born were in maintained primary schools as rising-fives. This would include some already in nursery classes. The corresponding figure for the ILEA was 56 per cent. There is undoubtedly great variation from place to place but, bearing in mind that the percentage is tending to rise slightly, it seems reasonable to reckon that at present about three-quarters of the spring rising-fives are in school in January, in the country as a whole.

3. We are much more in the dark about the percentage of summer-born children in school as rising-fives, since the Department of Education and Science has not hitherto collected detailed information on summer rolls. The *Where* survey (page 81) showed that a fair number of LEAS *aim* to admit rising-fives in the summer as well as in other terms; others do this provided that additional staff are not required; others again expect them all to wait until September.

It is rare for Plowden to misinterpret its own statistics, but this does happen in para. 351 where it is shown that, of a small sample of children entering infant school after Easter 1964, 66 per cent entered as rising-fives. This is interpreted as meaning that 66 per cent of the summer-born were able to enter school as rising-fives; what it actually means is that the ratio of summer-born to spring-born among the summer entrants was 66:34. However, if we then assume that about 25 per cent of the spring-born were left over to enter in the summer term, we can calculate from this ratio that about 35 per cent of the summer-born entered as rising-fives. The sample was however rather small.

In the ILEA in summer 1969, 28 per cent of the summer-born were in school. Bearing in mind the rather lower spring percentage for the ILEA, compared with the whole country, this suggests that over-all a proportion of about one-third of the summer rising-fives attending school may be a reasonable guess.

ORIGIN OF THE LONDON PLAN

In the autumn of 1968 leading members of the ILEA became very concerned about the handicapping of the summer-born. Lady Plowden, a co-opted member of the Authority, was influential in alerting them to this problem. Two short-term proposals were accepted in principle for discussion with representatives of the London teachers: (a) the possibility of half-time admission of rising-fives in the summer term so that more of them could gain school experience during that term; (b) the Southampton scheme for children to join pre-entry groups during the term before full-time entry. Both of these short-term proposals, which have been discussed in more detail in chapter 2, were later put to head teachers in London to be implemented or not at their own discretion.

It was realised at the outset, however, that proposals such as these only touched the fringe of the problem. The whole pattern of early schooling might need to be looked at again. Plowden had done this, but the two Plowden proposals might not be the only ones meriting consideration. It was realised that, if any longer-term proposals involved a change in the statutory age of admission, this would require legislation; but a new education bill, dealing with a variety of matters might soon be in preparation; this could, perhaps, include permissive clauses giving local authorities the opportunity to experiment. However, the first step was to take a new look at the merits of various admission proposals, and a paper was requested which would provide a basis for discussion. It fell to me to undertake this review in consultation with other members of the primary team of the ILEA Inspectorate, and with members of the administration.

The first step was to prepare detailed descriptions of the four 'Plowden-type' admission proposals already in existence. These included the original proposal of the LCC Inspectorate working party, put forward early in 1964, the plan submitted by the LCC in its evidence to Plowden (see pages 97–9), and the *Long-term* and *Interim* proposals of the *Plowden Report* itself. An analysis was made of the implications of each plan for the three term-age-groups, and of the average age of entry to school and to full-time education. For each plan also, a theoretical exercise was undertaken, on the lines described on page 109 to find, for schools of various-sized intakes, what would be the requirements in staffing and accommodation. Much of this, indeed, had already been done, for the two LCC schemes in 1964, and for the Plowden proposals soon after the Report appeared.

It was now possible to make a close comparison of the educational merits of the four schemes and also of their practicability if, in the first instance, only modest increases in manpower and other resources were possible. The discussion made use of some of the twelve criteria, now listed explicitly in pages 89–92, and some of the merits and defects of the various plans, specified in chapter 4, were identified. In the discussions which followed, both with ILEA colleagues and with outside experts, we were gradually feeling our way towards a combined plan which would enhance the merits and offset the defects of any one plan. In the process, several variations, chiefly on the *Plowden Long-term Plan*, were investigated in some logistic detail and then discarded. What we eventually arrived at—which later came to be called 'the London Plan'—was in no way, therefore, a brilliant improvisation out of nothing, but the result of a slow process of discussion, investigation and adaptation, by several minds, and owing much to the four earlier plans from which it derived.

In particular, the *London Plan* has much in common with the proposals (pages 97–9) submitted by the LCC in its evidence to Plowden. However, those proposals were in some respects a little rigid; Plowden taught us the value of flexibility at various points, and this feature of the two Plowden proposals has been incorporated in the *London Plan*. More important, the *London Plan*

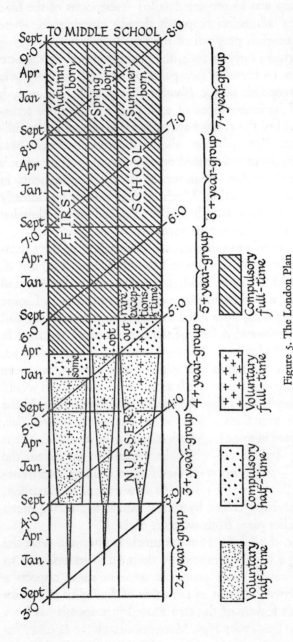

Figure 5. The London Plan

The Plowden percentages for half-time attendance have been distributed, as in figure 3, to give a rather higher proportion to the older, autumn-born children. The nursery stage would usually be associated with the first school. Transfer from first schools to middle schools is shown as occurring at 8+, but the Plan would be equally applicable if transfer was at 9+, or indeed with retention o the present 7+ infant/junior transfer age.

accepts the 'Plowden percentages' (page 101) for the maximum requirements of nursery education, part-time and full-time, as in the *Long-term Plan*. It aims to provide nursery education 'as thick on the ground' as infant education, and the achievement of this aim has been one of the criteria used in testing its practicability.

THE PLAN DESCRIBED

In reading the following description, the reader may find it helpful to refer to figure 5 on page 120, which is a flow-diagram similar to figures 2 to 4.

1. Full-time schooling would be compulsory for all children from the September after they reached the age of five and, for autumn-born children, also during the summer term preceding that September.

2. Half-time schooling would be compulsory for all children in the term preceding the normal compulsory date of entry to full-time schooling; i.e. half-time schooling would be compulsory for autumn-born children from the January after they became five, and for spring- and summer-born children after Easter.

These two compulsory requirements would, however, be applied with flexibility, in that there would be the possibility of exceptional children 'opting out' if a case could be made. Thus:

3. A summer-born child, who would be between 5:0 and 5:4 in September, would be allowed to attend only half-time in the autumn term, if the parents made a case acceptable to the LEA.

4. Exceptional children could also be excused the compulsory half-time attendance specified under (2) if the parents made a case acceptable to the LEA.

5. An LEA would be required to make voluntary half-time schooling available, before the age at which half-time schooling was compulsory, to as many as possible of the 3+ and 4+ year-groups, attaining, by a date to be arranged, provision for the Plowden percentages—35 per cent of the 3+ year-group and 75 per cent of the 4+ year-group.

6. An LEA would also be required to make voluntary full-time schooling available for some children below the age of compulsory full-time attendance, such provision to reach the Plowden percentage of 15 per cent for each of the 3+ and 4+ year-groups by a date to be arranged.

7. Classes which only contained children of present infant age (i.e. rising-fives and upwards) would be in classes of normal infant standards of roll and accommodation applying at the time. On the other hand, where a class contained *any* children below this age, it would be organised on nursery standards of roll, accommodation and nursery assistance.

8. All classes would be under the direct control of a qualified teacher.

The implications of the Plan for the three term-age-groups are shown below. I have made the same assumption as I made (page 101) in the case of the Plowden nursery proposals, that a higher proportion of the children who are old within the year-group will attend voluntarily half-time at 3+, and that the 35 per cent so attending will in fact be made up of some 55 per cent of the autumn-born, 35 per cent of the spring-born and 15 per cent of the summer-born. I have also assumed in the following table that the full percentage of an age-group, expected to attend voluntarily, will in fact attend from September, though in practice some may start later in the year. The 'opting out' provided for in (3) and (4) above has not been allowed for, since it seems likely that quite a small proportion of children will make use of it.

Autumn-born
Voluntary half-time (55%) or full-time (15%) at 3:8—4:0 in September.
Voluntary half-time (75%) or full-time (15%) at 4:8—5:0 in September.
Compulsory half-time in January at 5:0—5:4, if not already full-time.
Compulsory full-time after Easter at 5:4—5:8.
Average age of entry to school = 4:3; to full-time = 5:2.

Spring-born
Voluntary half-time (35%) or full-time (15%) at 3:4—3:8 in September.
Voluntary half-time (75%) or full-time (15%) at 4:4—4:8 in September.
Compulsory half-time after Easter at 5:0—5:4, if not already full-time.
Compulsory full-time in September at 5:4—5:8.
Average age of entry to school = 4:1; to full-time = 5:1.

Summer-born
Voluntary half-time (15%) or full-time (15%) at 3:0—3:4 in September.
Voluntary half-time (75%) or full-time (15%) at 4:0—4:4 in September.
Compulsory half-time after Easter at 4:8—5:0, if not already full-time.
Compulsory full-time in September at 5:0—5:4.
Average age of entry to school = 4:0; to full-time = 4:10$\frac{1}{2}$.
The weighted* overall average age of entry to school is 4:1$\frac{1}{4}$ and to full-time 5:0$\frac{1}{3}$.

There are certain broad features that are worth noting about this general pattern before we get down to a detailed analysis of its merits.

In the first place, the amount of deferment of the statutory age for compulsory full-time attendance is quite small—one term in the case of the autumn- and spring-born and not at all in the case of the summer-born.

Secondly, the ideal pattern of half-time before full-time is achieved for all children—except for a few of those who opt out and for the 15 per cent for whom full-time schooling from 3+ is deemed to be necessary. Apart from these, all children have at least one term of half-time schooling before becoming full-time, and it will be shown that, on average, children attending half-time do so for three and two third terms.

* The weighting is for relative numbers in term-age-groups.

Thirdly, under the *London Plan*, both the total length of school experience and the actual time spent in school, up to the age of 7+, would be greater than under present arrangements. Leaving aside the 15 per cent under the *London Plan* who would attend full-time from 3+ and those now attending nursery education, it can be shown that, under the *London Plan*, children would have, on average, some ten terms of school experience before 7+; if half-time attendance is only counted as half, this amounts to about eight terms actually in school. Under present arrangements, the comparable average figure on both counts is 7·6 terms.

Lastly, it is worth noting at this stage that summer-born children would enter school, on average, at a slightly earlier age than the others, so gaining some compensation for being young within the year-group.

EDUCATIONAL ASSESSMENT

Let us now look closely at the plan in relation to the twelve criteria discussed on pages 89–92, which we have already applied in our assessment of earlier Plowden-type proposals. I have given each criterion a short title to save the reader from constant reference back.

1. *Speed of implementation*

This is a point we shall examine in full detail in chapter 6. It will be shown, from studies of actual schools, that the plan could be operated to a very high degree with very little increase in present teaching staff and accommodation and that with no increase whatever in these resources, it could still be operated in large measure. This is not to say that the *London Plan*, like all other means of expanding nursery education, would not make considerable demands in the recruitment and training of nursery assistants. This factor will be assessed later. It would, however, be the only major factor limiting immediate implementation.

2. *Half-time before full-time*

The main finding on this point has already been given, that the 85 per cent not attending full-time nursery education from the start would have, on average, about $3\frac{2}{3}$ terms of half-time schooling before becoming full-time. More detailed findings for the three term-age-groups may be of interest. They can easily be calculated from the table on pages 122-3. It is assumed that the full percentage of an age-group expected to attend voluntarily, do so from September, and that opting out is negligible. The percentages given are of the total not in full-time nursery education:

Autumn-born
  65% have   5 terms half-time before full-time
  24% ,,   2 ,,   ,,   ,,   ,,
  12% ,,   1 term   ,,   ,,   ,,
Average ,, 3·8 terms

Spring-born
  41% have   6 terms half-time before full-time
  47% ,,   3 ,,   ,,   ,,   ,,
  12% ,,   1 term   ,,   ,,   ,,
Average ,,   4·0 terms   ,,   ,,   ,,

Summer-born
  18% have   6 terms half-time before full-time
  71% ,,   3 ,,   ,,   ,,   ,,
  12% ,,   1 term   ,,   ,,   ,,
Average ,,   3·3 terms   ,,   ,,   ,,

Weighted Year-group Average: 3·67 terms half-time before full-time.

It may seem at first sight that five or six terms of half-time schooling, for many children, is a long introduction. If it is thought of just as an introduction, as a smoothing of the transition from home, perhaps it is. However, if Plowden was right that some 50 per cent of children can benefit from schooling, usually half-time, beginning at 3+, but also that for many of them full-time schooling is a strain before five or five-and-a-half, then it follows that many will have as much as five or six terms half-time. But our figures can be taken as maxima. They assume, as we have seen, that every child included in the 35 per cent of a year-group, attending half-time at 3+, will attend from September, whereas in fact a good many may not start till January or after Easter, when many of them will be turned four—though they still count as 3+ since this was their age at the beginning of the school year. Of course, if some children do not attend from September, then classes could be smaller in the early part of the year, or a teacher might be saved or used in other ways.

3, 4. *Association and continuity between nursery and infant education*

For the foreseeable future, our present nursery schools would continue their separate existence, and some additional nursery centres might be built from time to time where a clear advantage in this arrangement could be seen. Our nursery schools have done much to maintain a consistent high standard of nursery education and nursery training and should continue to do so.

This separate nursery provision, old and new, would probably serve mainly to meet the needs of most of the 15 per cent requiring full-time nursery education—though one hopes with sufficient flexibility for some children to be accepted half-time, especially at first. However, the greater part of the nursery provision under the plan, especially half-time, would be in groups forming part of existing primary schools. This is inevitable, since the spare places for the youngest children attending half-time would become available through the deferment of compulsory full-time attendance.

But it is also, in my view, an excellent thing that the youngest infant classes should extend downwards into the nursery age-group.* We already have experience at Eveline Lowe Primary School† in London (designed by the DES Development Group in close consultation with Plowden's advisers) of some classes

---

* Nursery teachers will probably prefer to think of it the other way round as nursery classes extending upwards into the infant age-range.

† DES *Building Bulletin 36. Eveline Lowe Primary School, London* (HMSO 1967).

deliberately planned for vertical groups with an age-range of two or three years, so bridging the traditional gap between the nursery stage and the bottom of the infant school. Such an arrangement is beginning to be followed in some new schools elsewhere. This is not to say that many classes under the *London Plan* need have as wide an age-range as this. For example, in the study to be described later in which the *London Plan* was applied to the circumstances of forty actual schools, it was sometimes found possible in the larger ones to have a separate class for the children of 3+, especially where the school already has a nursery class. More often, however, the 3+ children and the younger members of the 4+ year-group would be together, giving an age-range of perhaps $1\frac{1}{2}$ years. Only in schools which at present have as few as two or three infant classes would it be common to have the complete range of 3+ and 4+ children, possibly with two or three of 5+, in one class. So the fear, sometimes expressed by infant teachers, that the *London Plan* would entail vertical grouping over the entire nursery-infant age-range is quite groundless, except possibly in the odd village school with a single infant class.

Nevertheless, a class containing children aged 3+ and 4+ at the beginning of the school year would quite definitely bridge the traditional gap between the nursery and infant age-groups. It would call for some adjustment on the part of both nursery and infant teachers and for in-service training directed more broadly towards work with young children than has been customary. This broadening of our approach would surely be a good thing and I shall have more to say about its possibilities in the final chapter. It is, to say the least, surprising that some horror and trepidation has been expressed on behalf of infant teachers—accustomed as they are to teaching rising-fives—that the *London Plan* might sometimes expect some of them to deal with some children about a year younger than this. One must hope that such hide-bound attitudes on the part of professional people will turn out to be rare, and that the majority of infant teachers, or at least those with a preference for the younger children, will rejoice in the opportunity to equip themselves to extend their range a little. Certainly most nursery teachers will welcome the chance to take some children through until they are 5+, as seems to be indicated in the NSA survey for Plowden (pages 96–7). It should be emphasised, however, that most infant classes will continue to be confined to children who are 5+ or 6+ at the beginning of the school year—or even older if there is a change to a first-school/middle-school type of organisation. There will, therefore, continue to be plenty of scope for infant teachers who prefer, on the whole, to teach the rather older children.

If every school containing infants had some nursery provision as well, this would have great advantages for parents. Nursery education would become a neighbourhood provision, available in the school just round the corner. This is particularly important if, as seems likely in the future, most nursery education is half-time, entailing for the mother four journeys for the sake of a half-day's schooling. Parents and teachers would welcome the continuity of home/school relationships, beginning often at 3+ and extending to 8+ at the very least. For the children there would be stability and continuity, both in their introduction to school and in learning. For head teachers there would be a great challenge to their professional understanding; they would need to see the vast possibilities opened up by an education of young children which was quite continuous from 3+ to 8+. Many, of course, are already faced with this challenge as an increasing number of schools containing infants have also a nursery class. Unfortunately, some infant heads treat their nursery class as very much a separate entity and opportunities for continuity are lost. This would rarely be possible under the *London Plan*, in which the classes for the younger children would tend to bridge the transition from nursery to infants. That this will involve, for some, the necessity and opportunity for some re-thinking about the education of young children will, in time, be accepted by teachers and educationists as a refreshing challenge.

5. Parental choice

The very wide range of choice which the plan offers to parents in starting a child at school is obvious from the description on pages 121–2 and the tables on pages 122–3 and 125. If there was a good case for a child to have full-time education from 3+, he would have a good chance of being among the 15 per cent for which this was provided, either in a separate nursery school or in the local primary school. More often, however, his parents would be happy for him to attend first half-time and such half-time schooling would be available to 35 per cent at 3+ and to 75 per cent at 4+ —and, indeed, for all 4+ children who had reached the age for compulsory half-time schooling. Some children might well benefit from full-time schooling at 4+ if they had begun half-time at 3+, so this is another pattern of entry which would sometimes be arranged, since there need be nothing sacrosanct about the equality of full-time provision, 15 per cent in both cases, suggested by Plowden at 3+ and 4+.*

The age and date at which a child entered half-time schooling would provide a further fine adjustment according to parental choice. Thus, although many parents would wish their children to attend from the September when they were 3+ or 4+, others might think their children not yet ready till later in the school year. Indeed, as we have seen, the length of half-time schooling could vary over a range from five or six terms down to the compulsory one term, and even from this one term there is the possibility, for good reason, of 'opting out'. There is, lastly, the further degree of flexibility, suggested by Plowden (para. 328), that some of the younger children might attend fewer than five sessions a week, and not stay for a whole session.

Finally, it must be admitted that in one respect parental choice may be limited in a way which is inevitable, but which some parents may not welcome. This is in regard to the choice of morning or afternoon session for half-time attendance. Experience of our present part-time nursery education shows that many mothers prefer their children to attend in the morning, often perhaps because they prefer to shop in the morning, delivering and collecting their children before and after. And yet, quite clearly, the morning and afternoon rolls of a part-time nursery class must be equal, within reason. Certainly it would not do, in

* Except, of course, that if a child is attending full-time at 3+, there must be a full-time place for him at 4+, but the converse is not true.

terms of standards, for the morning roll to exceed the maximum laid down. Nor will the plan work logistically if afternoon groups are *very* small. However, there is sufficient latitude in the operation of the plan to allow some variation. In the study of actual schools to be described later, it was found that quite often a group could be rather smaller than the maximum the standards allowed; where this was so, the afternoon group could be the smaller if this fitted in with parental choice. This is not, of course, a new problem, or in any way peculiar to the *London Plan*; it has had to be met already in our part-time nursery education, and will become widespread as part-time nursery education is extended by whatever means. The solution under the *London Plan*, as now, will lie in a great deal of mutual understanding between parents and schools, so that parents see the limits within which schools have to work, and schools appreciate and try to meet where they can the problems of parents.

6. *Some measure of compulsion*

Quite clearly there must be a 'statutory age' at which children must be in school, by law, full-time. Such a legal provision is necessary to give local authorities the power to enforce regular school attendance by children whose education might otherwise suffer through the negligence of parents; it is also necessary so that the statutory obligations of local authorities to provide education can be defined. In point of fact, the *London Plan* adopts two different statutory ages: the summer-born are required to attend full-time, as at present, from the beginning of the term following their fifth birthday; the autumn- and spring-born from the beginning of the term *after the term* following their fifth birthday. This may sound cumbersome, but legally it seems watertight enough; certainly the problem of definition is, if anything, easier than that presented by the two dates of the *Plowden Interim Plan* (pages 110–11).

However, the *London Plan* (like the *Plowden Interim Plan*) also includes a compulsory requirement for half-time attendance, and in the case of the *London Plan* this applies to all children except for those allowed to opt out) for the term before compulsory full-time attendance. Some doubt may reasonably be expressed as to whether this compulsory half-time requirement should apply to the summer-born who, as at present, will only be aged 5:0 to 5:4 on attending full-time in September. Should they be *required* to attend half-time during the preceding summer term when they would be only rising-fives and their attendance (full-time) under present arrangements is voluntary? In the case of these children we should, in fact, be pushing back a compulsory requirement (though only for half-time schooling) by one term. The LCC proposal to Plowden (pages 97–8) was content that these summer-born children should attend half-time in the summer if their parents wished it, and it was expected that places in sufficient number could be provided for them. This point was the subject of considerable discussion when the *London Plan* was in preparation. In the end we decided on compulsion on the following grounds:

i. If 'half-time before full-time' is in general the right pattern, it should be applied regardless of term of birth.

ii. The summer-born have only two years of full-time schooling before 7+ and are further handicapped by being young within the year-group, so could benefit even more than the rest from a previous term of half-time schooling and a gradual introduction to school.

iii. While it might be true that the majority of parents of summer-born children would welcome their attendance half-time in the summer term, there is a danger that ignorant and shiftless parents would not take the trouble to enter them voluntarily, so that many children who most needed this introduction to school would not get it.

iv. The compulsion to attend half-time is not absolute: there is provision, in approved cases, for 'opting out'.

These seemed to us good reasons for retaining this feature of the plan. On the other hand, it will be shown later that, when the implications of the plan were analysed in the actual circumstances of forty London schools, there were logistic advantages in certain cases if it was not considered essential for *every* summer-born child to be found a place in the summer term, when numbers tend to be high; in a few schools quite a small proportion of these children were sufficient to tip the balance towards the need for an extra room and an extra teacher. In some areas, speedy implementation of the plan might be helped if, in the first instance, there was only voluntary attendance of summer-born children during the summer term preceding their full-time attendance. There would then be the opportunity to consider further, in the light of experience, whether their attendance needed to be made compulsory, or whether such compulsion could be dispensed with. The point will be considered again on p. 161.

7. *The exceptional child*

This criterion suggests that statutory requirements, geared to the needs of the vast majority, need to be applied with some flexibility in the case of exceptional children, though under suitable safeguards. In other words, there should be provision for 'opting out' if a clear educational case for it could be submitted. It is worth noting that, as a means of dealing with exceptional children, 'opting out' is an alternative to attendance being voluntary, i.e. 'opting in'. If attendance is voluntary, parents who think that their children are exceptional in not being ready for school, will not send them. This, however, throws the entire onus of the decision on the parents—though they should be able to seek guidance if they wish. Sometimes their decision will be right and their children, quite genuinely, will not be ready for school. But sometimes it will be wrong; the parents, perhaps, being over-protective or negligent or ignorant; these children will then miss the benefit of school till a later age, together with those for whom there is a genuine case for deferment. This may not matter very much when children are very young and when the decision whether a particular child should attend nursery education is perhaps *best* made, in the majority of cases, by his parents. It is when children begin to approach the normal age to begin full-time schooling that the voluntary principle begins to break down; for the child of over-protective or negligent or ignorant parents may then, through non-attendance, suffer serious disadvantage. So there comes a time when, for the vast majority, attendance must be compulsory; but there must still be provision for the genuine exceptions, and it is here that 'opting out' retains an element of the voluntary principle, but with safeguards.

It was shown on page 121, (3) and (4), that the plan provides for two kinds of opting out:

i. Summer-born children may be given permission to attend half-time instead of full-time in the autumn term, when they would be, to begin with, aged only 5:0 to 5:4. It is to be hoped that such exceptions would be quite rare, since these children have the handicap of being young within the year-group. However, it may also be expected that most of these applications for opting out will be on fairly good grounds, since parents are not very likely through selfishness or negligence to land themselves with the slightly more troublesome half-way-house of getting the child to school half-time. Though their full-time schooling will thereby be shortened, these children will at least benefit from the right pattern of entry—half-time before full-time. If they also opted out of compulsory half-time schooling in the summer term, they will then only have the autumn term half-time before they become full-time in January. If not, they will get two terms of half-time schooling; indeed, the parents may have taken advantage of the opportunity for voluntary half-time schooling for them much earlier, and feel that this is the right pattern for them a little longer. In this way, some children opting out of the first term of compulsory full-time schooling might actually get *longer* school experience than some of their fellows; and this pattern of an extended entry to full-time schooling might be very appropriate for some children who were, perhaps, a little immature, but with an educationally stimulating home background. Incidentally, there should be no difficulty in the way of a child switching to full-time attendance at any point in the term if parents and teachers think he is ready. The fact that the child is already at school half-time would enable the head teacher to contribute good guidance on this point from her side.

ii. The second kind of opting out allowed for is for a child to be excused compulsory half-time attendance in the term before compulsory full-time schooling. It is difficult to gauge how often applications for this kind of opting out may be made. Some parents with little informed interest in their children's education may feel that half-time schooling is 'more trouble than it's worth' and so seek permission for opting out irrespective of the child's needs. In some other cases there may be real justification for some deferment of entry to school on grounds of immaturity, and these applications should be favourably considered. One disadvantage in opting out of this kind is that, at least for autumn- and spring-born children, it means that the first entry to school would be full-time. In such cases it might be well if administrators did not always insist on attendance being quite full-time in the first few weeks of compulsory full-time schooling.

The most usual grounds for giving permission for either kind of opting out would be the child's immaturity or insecurity, or ill-health of a kind which would make attendance, part-time or full-time, a serious strain. Immaturity may cure itself after a term's deferment, since the child will be that much older. Insecurity may arise from home difficulties which, coinciding with a child's entry to school, could have a most adverse effect, but which may pass. Ill-health may also be of a temporary nature—the child may have had a serious infection or operation shortly before he was due to enter school. If it is more chronic, the application to opt out may provide the occasion for it to be recognised and put right.

There will be some temptation to administrators to be over-generous in approving applications for opting out when there is great pressure of numbers at a particular school, perhaps in the summer term; this temptation should be resisted, and approval only given in cases where it seems clear that the child will benefit.

The precise machinery for applications and approvals may need to be worked out locally. Presumably the parents of children due, by law, to attend half-time or full-time would need to be given simple printed information of this and of the possibility of opting out for good reason, and of the procedure for making application. In the case of children already attending half-time, but whose parents wished them to opt out of full-time, the application could be channelled through the head teacher with her comments. In the case of children not yet in school, the application to be excused half-time attendance would be made to the local education office, and would be investigated in the first place by a school-welfare officer visiting the home. Where necessary, the views of the educational psychologist, the school doctor, or the child's own doctor, could be sought. Probably the number of applications would not be large, and cases presenting real difficulty quite rare; administratively, the matter might be as little time-consuming as some of the other decisions on individual children which now have to be taken—for example, in cases where early or late transfer to secondary school is sought for some special reason. In any case, there now seems wide agreement that some flexibility in statutory admission requirements ought to be provided; if so, the necessary machinery will need to be devised, whether for the *London Plan* or one of the alternatives. As parents in general become more aware of the purpose and value of a gradual entry to school, it is likely that applications to opt out will tend to become limited to instances which present no difficulty, since a clear case can be made.

Lastly, it is worth noting that, where a child is allowed to opt out from half-time attendance, it is all the more desirable that opportunities should be taken during that term for the child to become acquainted with the school in the ways suggested in chapter 2.

8. *Compulsory full-time schooling; later—but not much later*

Under the *London Plan*, the amount of deferment of the statutory age is small—one term for the autumn- and spring-born children, not at all for the summer-born. When we consider the actual opportunity to be admitted, the deferment is, of course, rather greater than this, since nearly all autumn-born children, many spring-born children, and some summer-born children are now admitted as rising-fives. The degree of deferment compared with present *practice* would therefore work out something like this, if we rely on the approximate estimates of rising-fives in school given on page 22:

Age-group	Proportion	Deferment
Autumn-born	virtually all	2 terms
Spring-born	a quarter	1 term
	three-quarters	2 terms
Summer-born	two-thirds	nil
	one-third	1 term

We have seen (pages 122–3) that the average age of entry to full-time schooling under the plan (including the 15 per cent in full-time nursery education at 3+) is: autumn-born—5:2, spring-born—5:1, and summer-born—4:10½. The weighted over-all average is 5:0⅓. It is impossible to calculate with quite the same precision the average age of entry to full-time schooling in our present maintained schools, including nursery education, but it almost certainly falls between 4:10 and 4:11. The comparison of averages is not, of course, very meaningful in such a context, but for what it's worth, we can say that the overall average deferment in entry to full-time schooling under the plan, when in full operation, would be of the order of half a term. Whatever weight we attach to this particular datum, we can certainly say that the plan meets the requirements of this criterion—'a little later, but not much later'.

9 and 10. *Reducing the birthday handicap*

We have seen that this at present operates in three ways:

    i. A variation of one year in length of infant schooling.

    ii. A variation of two terms in age of entry to full-time schooling.

iii. A variation of a year in age within the year-group. This cannot be altered; we can only seek to compensate for it.

One of the defects, as we have seen, of the *Plowden Long-term Plan* is that the single date of entry achieves uniformity in length of full-time schooling at the cost of *increasing* the variation in age of entry to it. The *London Plan* attempts a compromise: the variation in both respects is reduced to one term. Bearing in mind also the wide scope for parental choice which the Plan affords in length of half-time schooling, this seemed to us a very reasonable solution to these two aspects of the birthday handicap. In the nature of things, no complete solution is possible, but this seemed to approach it more nearly than any other proposal.

As to the third aspect of the birthday handicap: the plan provides some compensation to those who are young within their year-group, by enabling them to enter school, half-time and full-time, on average a little younger than the others do (pages 122–3) The differences are not large—up to about a term in both cases—but may be sufficient to have the necessary compensating effect.

11. *Stability of classes and staffing*

The 'shuffle-up' of some children from class to class during the year has already been mentioned (page 89) as a feature of present admission arrangements one would like to avoid as far as possible. The *London Plan* does not altogether escape it, but keeps it to quite small proportions. A close analysis has been made of the composition, term by term, of the classes for the younger children in the twenty schools in Peckham for which an application of the *London Plan* has been worked out. None of the 3+ children would need to move, but of the 1 500 children aged 4+, about 16 per cent were found to need* to change classes during the year, but only if any movement was limited to these younger children. If, instead, any movement between the younger classes was allowed to spread to and be partly absorbed by the older classes, as now

---

* The need mainly arises after Easter when a class or classes then consisting of rising-fives or over may need to expand up to normal infant numbers in order to accommodate children who will then be attending full-time.

usually happens, the average movement throughout the classes of present nursery and infant age would be nearer 5 per cent. This is certainly less than the movement now taking place in many infant schools in which vertical grouping (which reduces movement) is not used. The actual proportion changing classes would, in practice, be less than 5 per cent, for two reasons. Firstly, the Peckham analysis assumed that all 4+ children attending voluntarily half-time would attend from September, but a fair number may not, so giving latitude in class rolls at the beginning of the school year. It would then often be possible to plan the composition of classes at the beginning of the year in such a way as to avoid or reduce changes later. Secondly, there are in practice always children joining or leaving an infant school in the course of a year owing to family removals—sometimes in quite large numbers. Often this would mean that the new children could fill the gaps in a class of appropriate age-range, so that children already settled in another class need not move. It is difficult to quantify these factors, but it seems unlikely that in practice the percentage of children under 7+ who would be involved in a 'shuffle up' would, on average, exceed about 3 per cent.

Although change of class under the *London Plan* affects quite small numbers, any change of class for a child during the year, other than for educational reasons, is undesirable. As Plowden says (para. 772) 'the class, with its own teacher, should remain the basic unit of school organisation.' Nevertheless, recent developments involving the co-operation of classes and class teachers have reduced the significance of class membership, and made a change of teacher less traumatic. Certainly for those few children of 4+ who may need to move during the year, it will be an advantage if they have already had happy working relationships, on occasion, with the teacher who will be taking them on, perhaps just for the summer term, but in some cases continuing with them the following year.

Another aspect of stability is stability of staffing throughout the year. If additional teachers have to be used in the summer term, this can sometimes mean that their quality is not high, or that supernumerary teachers have to be diverted from their other duties to take a class, or that supply teachers have to be used who will then not be available to cover sickness vacancies—fortunately less frequent in the summer. Theoretical calculations suggest that the difference in number of infant staff required in the summer, as compared with autumn and spring, under present admission arrangements, may be of the order of 10 per cent. Similar calculations on the *London Plan* suggested that the increase required in the summer would only be about 3 per cent. The exercise in which the principles of the *London Plan* were tested against the actual circumstances of 40 London schools gave a still lower figure—0·5 per cent. However, this exercise was applied in two neighbourhoods under considerable pressure, where there was rarely room for an additional teacher to operate in the summer term. So, in my exercise, as in reality in these neighbourhoods, classes tended to rise to the maximum standard roll in the summer instead of the number of classes and teachers being increased. In easier circumstances, another class might sometimes be formed in the summer, with advantage, and this would in fact result in some variation in staffing over the year—though certainly much less than under present arrangements.

12. *Standards*

We come, finally, to the most crucial criterion of all—the maintenance of standards. It would be the height of dishonesty to claim to provide through the *London Plan* nursery education for all who wish it, if what in fact was provided was a mere travesty of nursery education—something akin, perhaps, to that provided in the 'baby rooms' of the early years of the century. The crux of the matter could lie in the attitudes of teachers. If they rise to the challenge of an education which is quite continuous from 3+ to 8+, we may well see the emergence of standards which transcend anything yet achieved in the education of young children. I shall have more to say on this theme in the final chapter.

Meanwhile, we must be content to assess the plan in terms of measurable standards, for example, pupil/teacher ratio and the area of accommodation per child. Clearly, the plan must not entail any worsening of either. Two standards, however, are involved: a nursery standard and an infant standard. In the application of the plan to the actual circumstances of forty London schools, described in chapter 6, nursery standards were applied to any class in which there were *any* children under rising-five in a given term. For such classes, 25 sq.ft per pupil was allowed—which means that if the room available for a class was of only 500 sq.ft, the roll was reckoned at twenty pupils, and so, proportionately, in other cases. But even where the room available was over 750 sq.ft, the limit of class roll for these younger children was set at thirty places*—the normal limit for a nursery class. On the other hand, in the case of classes consisting *only* of children of rising-five age or over, the average infant class roll of the school in question, in summer 1969, was taken as the standard roll for such classes. The accommodation limit for these children was the usual infant standard of not less than 10 sq.ft per pupil.

Three points are worth noting about these aspects of standards. First, it has been said that if a class contained *any* children under rising-five, it was allowed nursery standards. In some cases, the vast majority of a class might, in a given term, be rising-five or over; nevertheless they would benefit, as at present children of infant age do not, from the favourable staffing and accommodation of nursery standards. Secondly, it was found in practice that a fair number of classes containing younger children tended to be below the standard roll in the autumn and spring terms; this benefit could be concentrated on these classes or shared with some other classes by some adjustment of numbers. Thirdly, it is to be noted that a class on nursery standards will, of course, have a trained nursery assistant. The majority of the class may be of present infant age; it will still have a nursery assistant if it includes any children below this age. Some classes will all become of present infant age by the summer term, and will then be on infant

* Exceptions occur in the case of a few rooms being specially provided under the Urban Aid Programme, with accommodation of 1 000 sq.ft or more, in which a maximum nursery roll of forty has been officially approved, subject to the qualified teacher being assisted by *two* trained nursery assistants.

standards of accommodation and roll; nevertheless, in calculating the number of additional nursery assistants required, it was considered impracticable to engage a nursery assistant for the autumn and spring and not retain her for the summer term. So these children, though now of present infant age, would still benefit in this way.

I think it will be agreed that in these respects the standards adopted for children of present nursery age are in no way inferior to those which now apply, and that for the younger children of present infant age, the standards chosen are, on average, marginally better. However, there is another aspect of standards which should be considered. In my discussion of the *Plowden Long-term Plan* (page 103), the point was made that one qualified teacher supervising three groups of 20 could mean that she would be dealing with 120 children in the course of the day, if all were part-time. Some of the more important objectives of nursery education, it was suggested, could not possibly be attained if skilled professional guidance was spread so thinly. How does the *London Plan* come out on this point? Here again the studies of how the plan would work out in actual schools provide the answer. This further analysis has been done on the twenty Peckham schools, and there appears to be wide variation in the number of children a teacher must deal with in the course of a day. The number is small where the class is small and most of the children are full-time; it is larger where the children are mostly of an age to be on infant standards of roll, but where most are still half-time. The actual numbers of children to be dealt with in the course of a day, in the classes studied, range from 30 up to 74 children, with a median of 50. In addition, there is one class authorised for 40 in the morning and 40 in the afternoon under the Urban Aid Programme; already, under present arrangements, its teacher will need to cope with 80 children in the course of a day. The median of 50 under the *London Plan* compares favourably with the 60 part-time children now dealt with in a part-time nursery class of thirty places. Eleven classes (out of 41) exceed 60 children in the course of a day in, usually, only a single term. If, however, it was decided that a teacher should not be expected to deal with more than 60 children a day, this ideal could be achieved (with one exception) by quite a small reduction (9 per cent) in the number of 3+ children accepted.

And so we come to the end of our assessment of the plan in relation to the twelve criteria. Inevitably this has been done at some length, so that the assessment could be as precise and informative as possible, and in order to bring out some details of the working of the plan which would have obscured its main features in a first account. At the end of this long trek, it may be agreed that the plan scores quite well on every one of the criteria —certainly better on the whole than any of those that preceded it. In short, if our criteria are right, the *London Plan* is the best yet. Its only real defect is being, at first sight at least, a little complex— though less so than the Plowden *Interim Plan*. This is inevitable in any plan which avoids the crudity of admission by year-group, and considers instead the needs of children born at different times in the year. Flexibility and a large measure of parental choice add to the complexity; but no one, after Plowden, will say that they are not needed. Parents—and even teachers—will need to get used to an unfamiliar pattern; but experience of past educational changes suggests that parents are quite quick to adapt—provided that teachers and administrators take them into their confidence, and show them the reasons why—in terms of the well-being of their children.

| From Theory to Practice

It is one thing to make proposals which get the pattern of early schooling educationally right, and quite another to make them work with reasonable economy of teachers and accommodation. Yet, in a world where manpower and building resources are in short supply, such reasonable economy is a matter of some importance. As a matter of practical politics, it can make all the difference between action with a sense of urgency and pie in the sky.

Having reached, in the *London Plan*, what seemed to us the right pattern educationally, the next thing, clearly, was to find out if it could be achieved with the present number of teachers and rooms and, if not, what increases in both would be necessary. So I undertook a theoretical exercise in which the numbers of teachers and rooms required were calculated for a range of imaginary schools of different sizes. I shall not trouble the reader with the detailed findings since, in certain respects, the standards set differed a little from those used in the far more rigorous studies of actual schools presently undertaken. However, the results were quite encouraging. They suggested that the *London Plan* could be operated and achieve the full Plowden percentages of attendance, full-time and part-time, of 3+ and 4+ children, with quite small increases in teachers and rooms.

Some of my administrative colleagues were still not wholly satisfied; they made a suggestion which at first quite appalled me, since I knew the extremely lengthy, tedious and finicking labour which it would entail. But their suggestion turned out to be extremely valuable. They asked me to undertake a study of the feasibility of applying the plan to the circumstances, in 1969, of forty actual schools—with many of which I was very familiar. The task really involved finding out and then putting together two sets of facts. For each school I had first to find out, in complete detail, its accommodation: the number of rooms, the size of each, their arrangement; and also the authorised staff. Then I had to analyse the current roll in such a way as to arrive at the average year-group thrown up by the school's catchment area, dividing it into term-age-groups. Then, according to the principles of the plan, the children had to be fitted to the rooms: age-group by age-group, child by child, class by class, term by term; and bearing in mind all the time the sizes of the various rooms and the standards laid down by the plan for children of this age or that. It proved, indeed, to be a tedious undertaking, arithmetically of the simplest kind, but maddeningly beset with pitfalls, because of the number of factors to be considered together. I have described this more than once as a 'theoretical exercise'; and so it was, in the sense that only in theory were we gathering up all the children from 3+ upwards in a school's catchment area and arranging them in classes according to the principles of the plan. Nevertheless, all the data were known facts about actual schools, and the operation was closely akin to that which a headmistress might undertake in her study when arranging the composition of her classes for the coming year.

The methods and results of these studies of actual schools are given in some detail in the appendix; here we must be content with a broad outline. The two areas chosen, Peckham and Brixton, are of course both densely-populated urban areas, for the most part housing working-class families. Peckham was chosen because it was thought to be fairly representative of Inner London in the degree of pressure on school accommodation—though in fact, in the course of the study, it became clear that many of the schools were very full. So to use the results in Peckham as an indication for Inner London as a whole may, if anything, weight the scales slightly against the plan. Similarly, the pressure on school accommodation in Inner London appears to be rather greater than in England and Wales as a whole, judged by the percentage of rising-fives who can be accepted (pages 116-7). It follows, that if the plan will work in Peckham, it should work at least as well in the country as a whole.

On the other hand, it also seemed desirable to assess any difficulties the plan would encounter in a neighbourhood with quite exceptional problems. Brixton was chosen as an extreme example, a neighbourhood in which the rapid expansion of the large immigrant population had much exceeded official forecasts, so that, for the time being, finding places for the children in school was quite a serious problem. If the plan would work in Brixton, it should work anywhere in the country.

We have already seen in the last chapter that these detailed studies of the working of the plan in actual schools provided a mine of information on various points of some importance; for example, the number of children under the care of a teacher in the course of a day and the amount of transfer from class to class in the course of a year. However, the main objects of the exercise were three-fold:

1. To discover how far in these forty actual schools the compulsory requirements of the plan (page 121, (1) and (2)) could be met with present accommodation and staffing.
2. If, in any of the schools these compulsory requirements could not be met entirely, to find what additions to present accommodation and staffing would be needed so that they should be fulfilled.
3. When these additions had been made, to discover to what extent the Plowden maximum percentages requiring nursery education, half-time and full-time, would be met.

The results of the Peckham study were very encouraging. There were only two schools out of the twenty in which the compulsory provisions of the plan could not be fulfilled completely with existing accommodation and staffing. In these two, not all of the summer-born children could be given half-time places in the summer term before they entered full-time in September—as indeed most of them now do—at 5:0—5:4. As a proportion of the summer-born in all twenty schools, this short-fall in the two schools only amounted to $7\frac{1}{2}$ per cent. However, if 'half-time before full-time' is a compulsory requirement, there must be provision to meet it in every school. It was therefore assumed that an additional classroom (of 540 sq.ft), and an additional teacher, would need to be provided in each of these two schools, and the results now to be given take account of this small additional provision.

In the following table, the percentages of each year-group, averaged over the year, who could be placed in school, are given, with the corresponding Plowden percentages in brackets in each case:

	3+	4+
Full-time	2% (15%)	16%* (15%)
Half-time	38% (35%)	82% (75%)

It will be seen that the Plowden maximum percentages are actually *exceeded*, except in the provision for 3+ children full-time. This imbalance (if such it is) is easily accounted for. It needs to be realised that, in working out this exercise for a particular school, I often had some freedom of manoeuvre. If the accommodation looked ample, one might set aside from the first some full-time places for children of 3+, but the natural tendency was to work down through the term-age-groups from the 4+ to the 3+ children, and with some priority for half-time provision. However, one could not know at all precisely, until the whole operation had been completed for all twenty schools, just how it was going in overall percentage terms. It would then have been possible, of course, to repeat the whole operation again, in the hope of getting the final percentages just so, but this hardly seemed justified. †However, if it was felt strongly that the number

* The compulsory—i.e. 100 per cent—attendance of autumn-born children of 4+ in the summer term is, of course, not included in this figure.

† It might be supposed that the global figures could simply be adjusted by reducing those percentages which exceed Plowden's to the Plowden percentages, so increasing the 3+ full-time figure at the rate of one full-time place to every two half-time places reallocated. Unfortunately, in particular cases this does not

of full-time places for children of 3+ should be increased, there were several schools where this could easily have been done, at a cost of losing double the number of half-time places. Moreover, my analysis included two schools in which I accepted two-thirds of the 2+ year-group half-time from the term after they turned three. If they had not been accepted at this early age, the 3+ percentage, overall, could have been raised to 5 per cent. Finally, no allowance has been made for 'opting out' in the summer term when it would often make possible some increase in the full-time provision for children of 3+.

A further point ought to be considered. We have taken the 'Plowden percentages' very much for granted as the target to aim at, but I must myself confess to some doubts as to whether as many as 15 per cent of children are best suited by beginning their schooling full-time at 3+. Plowden had specially in mind, of course, children from homes which are in various ways inadequate, and the feeling was that such children were better in school throughout the day. The educational and social advantages of this, however, must be partly offset by the strain of attending school full-time at such an early age. One would think that, even for children from inadequate homes, it might often be best for them to begin school half-time at 3+ and to defer full-time schooling till 4+ when they would have considerable school experience behind them. If so, the pattern that has tended to emerge in this exercise, with rather less emphasis on full-time schooling for children of 3+, may be educationally right.

However this may be, it seems that, with the addition of the two rooms needed to operate the compulsory features of the plan, and with this one exception, the Plowden percentages can be more than achieved in the neighbourhood as a whole. This is

always work out. One runs into difficulties over the relation of class numbers to age-composition; or occasionally there may be room in autumn and summer, but not in the spring—and clearly a child cannot be accepted early in the year when there is no place for him later. Some of these difficulties might not arise in practice owing to the transfer of children in and out arising from family removal, but clearly, in a theoretical exercise, one cannot take account of this piece in the jigsaw. There can be no doubt that a detailed study school by school, is far more accurate than a global exercise, but it still has *some* limitations, of which this is one.

very far from saying that they can be achieved in the same degree at each individual school. There would be wide variation. In three schools, for example, there would be no room at all for children of 3+, whereas in five others all, or almost all, the 3+ children could be accepted from the beginning of the school year. Voluntary full-time provision would be limited to seven schools and the existing nursery school. So although every school could provide half-time schooling for virtually every child of 4+, throughout the year, the provision at 3+ and for voluntary full-time schooling would vary a good deal. We are already familiar with this kind of variation from school to school, for example, in the admission of rising-fives and in nursery provision. Under the *London Plan*, the degree of variation described above would be acceptable in the short run, in an urban area where the schools are not widely-scattered and the more ample provision well-distributed. But in the long run, one would like to see the more ample provision available everywhere, so that one can be sure that the individual needs of every child, whether for full-time or for half-time schooling, can be met in the school 'just round the corner'.

It may be agreed, however, that the results of this Peckham exercise are highly encouraging. This is true also, if we look at them another way, in terms of age of entry to school. The weighted overall average comes out at 4:1, which is marginally *better* than was calculated on page 123 from the Plowden percentages. On the other hand, the overall average age of entry to full-time schooling is $5:2\frac{2}{3}$—about two months later than was calculated on that page. This is due to the limited number of children of 3+ who, in the exercise, were accepted full-time, and is easily capable of some adjustment, as already shown.

How about the demands of the plan on teaching staff in these twenty schools? Here the results are particularly reassuring. Only 2 per cent more would be required than the number of infant and nursery teachers already serving in these schools in 1969. This is less than the present annual percentage increase in infant and nursery teachers employed by the ILEA. In other words, the use of just one year's increment in teachers of young children for this special purpose would, in the ILEA at least, enable the plan to be operated at the quite high level here described.

Moreover, we have left out of account the accelerated recruitment of part-time teachers which the plan would almost certainly encourage. To have one's own morning or afternoon group would be, for many part-time teachers, a more satisfying occupation than taking small groups extracted from many classes, as most of them do now. At present, part-time nursery classes are scattered sparsely, and the journey is a disincentive to some former teachers, who would be glad to take a morning or afternoon class if this was available close at hand. It may be, therefore, that not even a single year's increment in full-time teachers would be needed to get the plan well on its way.

I have discussed the results of the Peckham exercise in fair detail, since it can be taken as tolerably representative of urban areas throughout the country. If it differs from the average, then this is in the direction of Peckham schools' being under slightly greater pressure than most, so we are erring on the side of caution. On matters of costing, for example, we may not go far wrong in doing a proportion sum in order to get a rough idea of costs on a national scale.

However, there are also, throughout England and Wales, areas of exceptional difficulty, and a brief account of the similar study of twenty Brixton schools may be of interest to show how the plan fares under such conditions. Fuller details of this study are given in the Appendix.

In Brixton, as expected, the results were less favourable, though considerably better than we all feared when, perhaps with a certain touch of *schadenfreude*, my administrative colleagues invited me to tackle also this difficult area. However, there were here eight schools out of the twenty in which, without additional accommodation, it was not possible to provide half-time education for all the summer-born 4+ children during the summer term. As a proportion of the summer-born children in the twenty schools, about 27 per cent would be affected, going straight into full-time schooling in September at 5:0 to 5:4 (as most do now), without the advantage of at least a term of half-time schooling.

For each of these eight schools, therefore, it was reckoned that an additional classroom would need to be provided. With this addition, it was found that the percentages who could be placed were as follows (the corresponding Plowden percentages are again given in brackets):

	3+	4+
Full-time	0% (15%)	11% (15%)
Half-time	37% (35%)	89% (75%)

It would appear that my concern to achieve 'half-time before full-time' for the maximum number of children has again resulted in less full-time provision than many would think desirable. However, a reallocation of places to reduce the half-time percentages to the Plowden maxima would yield some full-time places, all of which could be allocated, if necessary, to the 3+ year-group, and the percentage for the 4+ year-group might be increased a little further when places released by 'opting out' were taken into account. The overall average age of entry to school, half-time or full-time, comes out at 4:1½, and of entry to full-time at 5:3½. Here again, a possible small adjustment to increase the percentages of full-time places, would also lead to some lowering of the average age of entry to full-time schooling. It was found that in Brixton the extra teachers required to staff the additional rooms would amount to 5·7 per cent of the nursery and infant staff at present employed. So, even in Brixton, with all its difficulties, the results of this exercise were not so very far short of the target, though at some cost in extra teachers and rooms.

WHAT WOULD IT COST?

The cost of an educational proposal has three main aspects. There is first the total cost in pounds and pence—the money that will have to be found for it out of rates and taxes. This is something which many progressive educationists are apt to view with fairly light hearts. After all, they would say, in our affluent society, an awful lot of money is spent on things which have little relation to the good life, or which are actually harmful. They would concede that politicians will inevitably feel some concern about the steady escalation of public expenditure, but this, they would say, is itself a matter of education of the public, in getting their priorities right.

The other two aspects are rather different; they concern manpower and building resources. Manpower of the level of ability required in teaching is in fairly short supply. It is true that some of it is now misused in occupations which, in a more sensible society, would have low social priority. Even so, to switch high-level manpower in a democracy not actually at war takes time; people have to be induced to change, not directed to do so, and training for a job like teaching is a lengthy business. Again, some building resources may be misapplied, but to switch their application in a society still sadly short of houses, hospitals, modern factories, and roads, again takes thought and time. And it is not as if much has not already been done to give education high social priority. Between 1964–5 and 1970–1, total education expenditure in money terms has nearly doubled, and its share of the gross national product has increased by 41 per cent.* Such figures signify already a substantial shift in the application of manpower and building resources. So costs are important: in terms of practical politics, in the light of other social priorities, and perhaps especially, in terms of the time it will take for an educational reform to be implemented.

It is obvious that to arrive at a really close estimate of the costs of the *London Plan* would require surveys on a nation-wide scale, a team of experts and a battery of computers. Here we can only attempt a very rough estimation, based on the study in Peckham and the use of a series of proportion sums. As we have seen, in terms of the pressure of numbers on school accommodation, Peckham may have rather more problems than the country as a

---

* K. Ollerenshaw, *Predictions of Education Expenditure* (*Local Government Finance*, May 1970).

whole. So in this respect, to argue from Peckham to the country as a whole is to err on the safe side. On the other hand, it is difficult, from a purely urban study, to be certain how the cost of the proposals would work out in small rural schools—of which there are still nearly 3 000 containing infants and with rolls of fifty or under.

There may, indeed, be other and larger sources of error. For example, although Peckham schools are under considerable pressure, they are also fairly well provided already with nursery accommodation; eight of the twenty schools have a nursery class now that the first phase of the Urban Aid Programme is completed, and there is also a small separate nursery school. This means that nursery provision in Peckham is already over double the national proportion in maintained schools. This will undoubtedly have been a factor favourable to the results of the Peckham study. It also means that a proportion of the costs of the proposal in nursery assistants and special nursery facilities will already have been incurred and that the *additional* costs may therefore be proportionately greater in areas less well provided already with nursery places. This can be allowed for, so far as the cost of nursery assistants is concerned. Otherwise, perhaps the best we can do in this preliminary study, is to acknowledge these sources of error, positive and negative, and hope that very roughly they cancel out.

We proceed, then, to our proportion sums. The ratio of an infant year-group in the twenty Peckham schools to an infant year-group in all the maintained primary schools in England and Wales is almost exactly[1] one to five hundred. If, therefore, we multiply the estimated costs in Peckham by five hundred, we should arrive at some idea of the cost of implementing the plan on a national scale. Any such estimate may well seem unrealistic through the action of inflation, even by the time this book appears. The same would apply, however, to nursery expansion by any other means, so a cost comparison should remain significant.

In considering the costs of an educational proposal, it is usual to draw a distinction between *Maintenance* or *Revenue Expenditure*— for example, salaries and consumable equipment costs, which have to be met every year, and, on the other hand, *Capital Expenditure*, needed once and for all in order to get the proposal under way. We shall therefore consider the costs of the *London Plan* under these two headings.

Maintenance expenditure

(i) *Teachers' salaries.* We can calculate[2] that on a national scale about 1 200 extra nursery and infant teachers would be required. Nursery and infant teachers tend to be young members of the profession, not yet on their maxima, and often without graduate or other special allowances. If we reckon about £1 700 per annum per teacher for salary, superannuation, etc., we shall be near the mark on scales as they stand at the time of writing. So the total cost for teachers would amount to about £2 000 000.

(ii) *Salaries of nursery assistants.* Every class in the Peckham exercise has been examined to see if it would rate a nursery assistant. The standard adopted was the generous one that a class would require a nursery assistant throughout the year if, at *any* time in the year, it included *any* children under rising-five. On this basis, the twenty schools would require between them 30 nursery assistants in excess of those now employed. However, at this point it seems fair to take into account that Peckham is rather well provided with nursery education and so with nursery assistants. An approximate allowance can be made for this, taking into account the number of nursery assistants (2 900) employed in England in 1967 (Plowden, table 37). When this is done, it seems that about 36 additional nursery assistants might in fact be required in the twenty schools, if in this respect they were strictly representative. Multiplying by 500, we arrive, therefore, at an additional requirement for the country as a whole of the order of 18 000. At a very rough estimate,[3] the total cost in salary and superannuation of a trained nursery assistant is, on average, about £700 a year, so the national cost on this count would be of the order of £13 000 000.

This cost, in money terms, of additional nursery assistants is quite modest; what is far more important for the rate of implementation of the plan is the cost in manpower. Nursery assistants are recruited from women of a level of ability for which there are many other demands. At present, NNEB training takes two years, though Plowden has suggested that suitable mature students should be allowed to qualify through a special one-year course. In either case, a good deal of the training time is, or would be, spent in schools. Until recently, this practical experience has been limited to nursery schools (not nursery classes); and there has sometimes been difficulty in finding enough nursery schools in which students could practise, so there has been something of a vicious circle. Now, however, some students are being allowed to do some of their practice with the reception classes of infant schools; this is in line with the blurring by the *London Plan* of the distinction between nursery and infant work, and should make it easier for the larger number of nursery assistants to be trained. However, the problem is much smaller than that envisaged in the *Plowden Long-term Plan*, which requires, as we have seen, about 85 000 nursery assistants when the full provision is complete in the 1980s. This is because, under the *Long-term Plan*, the day-to-day charge of a nursery group of twenty is not the direct responsibility of a teacher, but of two nursery assistants, so the total numbers required are large.

The rate of progress envisaged by Plowden (table 37) in the early stages of its programme for the training of nursery assistants is relevant to our problem. Starting from the 1967 number of 2 900 nursery assistants, it was estimated that this would remain the same in 1968, and then, as training courses multiplied, rise in the following way: 1969—5 600, 1970—9 300, 1971—12 700, 1972—16 400, 1973—22 100, and so on, at an increasing rate, reaching 71 700 by 1979. The relatively slow initial build-up arose from the fact that Plowden gave first priority in recruitment and training to teachers' aides. If, however, the present resistance of the teachers' associations to the use of teachers' aides is maintained, it should be possible to make more rapid progress in the supply of nursery assistants, perhaps reaching our target of 18 000 within about four years.

(iii) *Cost of training nursery assistants.* Plowden estimates (para. 1053) that if teachers' aides and nursery assistants together are recruited in the early years at a rate of 12 000 a year, the annual cost of their training would be about £5 000 000. No doubt it would not be necessary to maintain recruitment and training of nursery assistants at quite this rate in later years simply in order to make good 'wastage'. Even so, bearing in mind rising costs, it may be reasonable to set down an annual figure of £5 000 000 for this purpose.

(iv) *Cost of additional equipment.* The number of children (in full-time equivalents) in a school under the *London Plan* would be virtually the same as at present, since the additional places, mostly half-time, for the younger children, are found as a result of deferment of full-time schooling. Nevertheless, there would be some additional costs, mainly in order to extend the range of equipment in every school so as to cater for children of nursery age. It is difficult to quantify this item; but if we reckon roughly that a whole year-group of younger children needs to be catered for, and allow £2 a head for additional equipment, then the cost in Peckham would be £3 000, and for England and Wales, £1 500 000. Let us call it £2 000 000 to be on the safe side, but bear in mind that much of this cost would be in the first year or two when the main change-over in equipment was taking place.

We arrive, therefore, at an annual cost of maintenance of roughly £22 000 000. The last two items would not, however, need to be maintained, after the first year or two, at their high initial rate. Perhaps, therefore, a reasonable figure when the scheme was established would be of the order of £20 000 000, to which we shall need to add debt charges on capital expenditure.

Capital expenditure

(i) *Additional classrooms.* We have seen that, in Peckham, two additional classrooms would be required. The size allowed for was 540 sq.ft, largely because it was at first thought that temporary classrooms might be used which are available in this size. On nursery standards, such a classroom would take 22 pupils. However, washing and lavatory provision under immediate supervision would need to be available, and to provide a built-on classroom with these facilities, for 22 pupils, would cost anything up to £8 000. It is, of course, possible that collaboration of DES architects with a consortium of the large firms now specialising in classroom extensions, might come up with something decidedly cheaper, if a large programme of nursery expansion was set in motion. However, let us reckon that the two extra classrooms needed for our twenty schools would cost £16 000. On a national scale we therefore arrive at some £8 000 000 for this item.

(ii) *Sanitary adaptations to existing rooms.* Children of below rising-five require small w cs and wash-basins, so arranged that their use of them is easy for the nursery assistant to supervise. The standard is a w c and a wash basin for every ten children. Plans of the twenty schools were studied to see where these might go and roughly what they might cost. The need had been borne in mind in selecting the rooms to be used by the younger children and there were few cases in which finding a place for the sanitary provision would entail building outwards. In two cases the classes which would contain younger children were already well provided for, and only in two schools did two rooms require to be equipped. In two other cases the sanitary provision was already there and only access for immediate supervision needed to be provided. It is quite impossible to estimate the cost of these improvements at all precisely without architects' visiting the schools, but a rough but generous estimate might be an average cost per school of £2 000. On this basis, we arrive at £40 000 for the twenty schools, or £20 000 000 for the country as a whole.

(iii) *Furniture.* Since the number of children in school at a time would be virtually the same as at present, many items of furniture, not closely related to the age of the children, could continue to be used. There would, however, be need for some furniture, especially tables and chairs, to be replaced by sizes suitable for children of nursery age, though the replaced items could still be used elsewhere. Bearing this in mind, it is probably sufficient to allow £10 a place. If we reckon that there will be roughly one year-group of children in school at a younger age than at present, but that most of them will be half-time, the net needs of some 800 places have to be met, giving a cost of £8 000, or £4 000 000 for the country as a whole.

Adding up these three items of capital expenditure, we find that they total about £32 000 000. In the case of voluntary schools, some of this cost would be borne by the Church authorities. In practice, also, LEAs would find their share of the capital cost by borrowing, the debt charges at about 9½ per cent being added to the revenue expenditure. In all, therefore, we arrive at a total revenue cost in the early years, including debt charges, of about £25 000 000 a year, with some slight reduction to come in later years.

This is not chicken-feed. Still, it is quite a modest expenditure to provide nursery education for all who want it, while at the same time getting the initial pattern of primary education right for our children. It amounts, indeed, to an addition of only about 2 per cent to the predicted total revenue expenditure on maintained primary and secondary schools in 1971–2.*

THE COST OF OTHER SCHEMES

It is worth while to compare the cost of the *London Plan* with that of providing a comparable expansion of nursery education by other means. The Plowden nursery proposals were estimated (tables 40, 41) to cost nearly £60 000 000 a year when provision was complete. This was at 1966 prices; already, rising salaries of nursery assistants would add some £20 000 000 to this estimate.

We can also attempt a comparison with the cost of providing a large expansion of nursery education by the traditional means of creating new nursery schools and classes while leaving the present pattern of infant education unchanged. Only a very rough computation can be attempted. For the sake of simplicity, let us suppose that part-time nursery education is to be provided for 75 per cent of children, for one year, on average, before the present average age of entering infant schooling (i.e. at an average age of 3:11), and also that full-time nursery education is to be

---

* Ollerenshaw, K. (1970) The predicted amount is £1 321 000 000.

provided for 15 per cent of children at the same average age. Such a provision would lay more emphasis on part-time nursery education than we find, as yet, in current practice, but it would be both economical and in line with probable future development. On this basis, we can calculate[4] that about 360 000 extra places (full-time equivalents) would be needed. If, to simplify matters, we reckon that all of these would be in nursery classes of 30, it appears that about 12 000 rooms, 12 000 teachers and 12 000 nursery assistants would be required. The capital cost* would be that of building (or adapting) and furnishing 12 000 classrooms at perhaps an average of £10 000 apiece, a total of some £120 000 000. The annual cost* for salaries of teachers and nursery assistants and for equipment, but without reckoning additional training costs, would be about £30 000 000, plus debt charges in excess of £11 000 000 a year. This is a very rough computation, but it is clear that the annual cost would be more than half as much again as that of the *London Plan*, but very much less than the cost of the Plowden nursery proposals.

But money cost is not the main point. What stands in the way of a *rapid* expansion of nursery education on traditional lines is the large number of teachers of young children to be recruited and trained, and the very heavy demands on scarce building resources to give them a place to work. It must be emphasised, however, that this kind of cost comparison, persuasive though it may be, is not the main reason for seeking an alternative solution; the main reason is to get the best pattern of early education for our children.

PAYING FOR NURSERY EDUCATION?

An important Note of Reservation to the *Plowden Report* proposed a parental contribution to the costs of nursery education. It was signed by eight members of the Plowden Council, including Lady Plowden herself, Professor Ayer, Professor Donnison,

---

* These are minima, since the provision, especially in small rural schools, could not always be in the neat, economical groups of thirty that this rough calculation assumes.

and Dr Michael Young. A standard charge of 25p a half-day to meet running costs was suggested, but with remission of the charge for families with low incomes or several children. It is argued that nursery education is voluntary and that it is inequitable that parents who do not choose to use the facilities should have to pay through rates and taxes for those who do. (This argument could of course be used in relation to some other free facilities provided at the public expense, e.g. parks.) It is noted that in many other countries, including USSR, a charge is made for nursery education. But the main argument employed is that to finance an expansion of nursery education in this way would increase the chance of its being provided, not only for the children of parents who can pay, but for those of less fortunate parents also. However, it has already been shown that the main deterrent to the rapid expansion of nursery education is not money, but manpower and building resources, and this would be unaffected by a parental contribution. Moreover, there might be a real danger that some parents who were rather indifferent to their children's education, but who were outside the categories eligible for remission of the charge, might be swayed by the existence of a charge against taking the trouble for their children to attend half-time, at an age when this was voluntary. For these reasons, I would be reluctant to see the inclusion of a charge for voluntary attendance under the *London Plan*—though at the rate suggested in the Report this would more than cover the cost. On the other hand, if a charge would make the plan practical politics in the present climate, it could always be knocked off later. As with the Health Service, the vital thing is to get the pattern right.

THE MACHINERY OF CHANGE

The legislative and administrative procedures through which, step by step, an educational reform is brought to fruition is a matter for experts, of whom I am not one. However, even an amateur in such matters can see some of the possibilities and problems. Any Plowden-type proposal would require legislation to enable the statutory age of full-time attendance to be raised, or for half-time schooling to be legally acceptable at the present statutory age.

Such legislation could, however, be either mandatory or permissive. If it were mandatory, the new statutory arrangements would have to be applied by all local authorities from a given date. If it were permissive, LEAs would be *enabled*, from a given date, to raise the statutory full-time admission age, but would not be *required* to do so. The position would be analogous to that created by the Education Act of 1964, which enabled LEAs to establish middle schools with a later age than 11+ for transfer to secondary education. LEAs were thereby permitted to experiment with new patterns of school organisation at that stage, but were not required to do so; in practice, most have been content to retain a transfer age of 11+.

There is, perhaps, much to be said for new legislation concerning the statutory admission age to be permissive rather than mandatory. There are, after all, several Plowden-type proposals to be considered—not to mention the proposal for a *reduction* in the statutory age submitted by the NUT in its evidence to Plowden. I am naturally of the opinion that the *London Plan* is the best yet, and hope I may have persuaded the reader to a like opinion. Nevertheless, we may not yet know all the answers. Too often, in the past, educational thinking has been crystallised prematurely into mandatory legislation, when permissive legislation would have enabled local authorities to experiment and so, between them, find the best pattern. It is even possible that some variation might continue indefinitely, one pattern being right for one area, and a slightly different pattern for another.

If the new legislation were permissive, a local authority wishing to raise the age of full-time attendance (within limits laid down by the new Act), would be required, when seeking permission to do so, to submit also its proposals for extending the provision of nursery education. These would have to be acceptable to the Secretary of State before permission to raise the statutory age could be granted. This would ensure that alternative admission policies were submitted to nationally-informed scrutiny, and serve as a check on those few LEAs which might be tempted to raise the statutory age without making adequate provision for the extension of education of a high enough standard, in the opposite direction. In this way there would be opportunity for experiment with different patterns (though under central guidance), and to do this with the statutory backing of the Education Act, exercised through the powers of approval or rejection of the Secretary of State. There would be the further advantage that matters of detail would not need to be incorporated in the Education Act itself. After all, the *London Plan* does entail, as we have seen (page 121), a different statutory age for the autumn- and spring-born on the one hand and the summer-born on the other, and there are other matters of detail such as the definition of school terms, and the regulations relating to opting out. It should be possible for such details to become matters of agreed local regulation, rather than that they should clutter up the Education Act itself.

The possibility has already been mentioned of operating the plan in two steps, in the first of which the attendance half-time of summer-born children in the summer term before full-time entry would be voluntary. Compulsion would then be introduced later if, in practice, this was found to be necessary, because a fair number of children were missing this introduction to school without good reason. Phased implementation of this kind would mean that those schools—only two in Peckham—which could not accommodate quite all the summer-born children that term, would not be obliged to do so at once, but the LEA would be required to provide accommodation for their 100 per cent attendance, compulsory or voluntary, by a date to be arranged. Such flexibility in the early stages might encourage authorities to make a quick start, even though the full implementation of the plan in all schools might take several years. The effects of such a phasing of the scheme on the Plowden percentages are discussed in the appendix.

It would certainly take three or four years, after permissive legislation had been passed, for the scheme to get really under way. The expansion of training courses for nursery assistants would take time and there would also be sanitary improvements to be put in hand and carried out. Meanwhile, schools would begin to modify their admission practice so that children who, at present, are admitted full-time at rising-five were admitted only to half-time schooling. In the case of autumn- and spring-born children, they would continue half-time for the term after they became five. As a result, places would begin to become available for children to be admitted half-time before they were rising-five, and this could be done as the necessary nursery facilities, including nursery assistants, became available. No child, of course, who had already started school full-time, would be expected to change to half-time; thus the new pattern would be achieved gradually. Meanwhile, an intensive programme of parental education would be desirable, so that parents came fully to understand the purpose of the changes and the benefits they would offer to their children.

When the two-phase programme that has been suggested had been completed, largely with existing resources, this would not, one hopes, be the end of nursery expansion. In the first place, there might still be some need for expanding provision for full-time nursery education from 3+, so as to attain Plowden's 15 per cent—if, perhaps in particular areas, this was thought to be desirable. Possibly even more important, there should be sufficient elbow-room in every school for the full Plowden percentages to be attained everywhere, in order that parental choice and children's needs can be fully met in every small neighbourhood, in 'the school just round the corner'. This greater latitude in accommodation may be something which will come automatically in many areas if the recent small reduction in the birth-rate continues. If not, it will be an objective to be reached—not too slowly, one hopes—as the years go on.

Even when maintained nursery provision is available everywhere on this generous basis, there may still be some place for voluntary effort. It has already been suggested that some children, mainly three-year-olds, may find a small playgroup, attended perhaps only one or two mornings a week, a good introduction to school, especially if some of the other children and adults are known to them. To some mothers too, helping in a community venture of this kind may be a satisfying form of service, and with the added value to the community of extending the range of adults actively interested in education. Such a venture will not flourish in all neighbourhoods, and a generous provision of maintained nursery education will diminish the need which fostered the growth of playgroups. Nevertheless, it is to be hoped that the playgroup movement will continue to get some official support, for it is a healthy development both for mothers and children, and should continue to have some place in the long-term pattern for the education of young children.

NOTES

1. For the purposes of the Peckham calculations the size of a year-group in a school was taken as the average of the numbers of children of 5+ and 6+ (September ages) in the school in January 1969. For the twenty Peckham schools the total of these averages was 1499. In England and Wales the corresponding total was 772 224 (*Statistics of Education* 1969, table 6). The ratio of the Peckham to the England and Wales numbers was 1:515. It seems reasonable to round this down to 1:500, bearing in mind the falling numbers under five in the next few years and the approximate nature of the financial estimates.

2. In the Peckham exercise, $2\frac{1}{2}$ extra teachers were required for the full implementation of the compulsory aspects of the plan. This gives 1 250 for England and Wales. The $2\frac{1}{2}$ teachers represented 2 per cent of the nursery and infant teaching staff in Peckham. The total number of nursery and infant teachers in England and Wales (in full-time equivalents but excluding head teachers) was approximately 57 000 in January 1969 (table 1). Two per cent of this is 1 140. Splitting the difference between the figures arrived at by these two routes we arrive at 1 200.

My estimate of about £1 700 as the average total salary cost of an additional nursery or infant teacher is based on official estimates of the cost of the additional nursery teachers to be employed by the ILEA in 1971–2, corrected to allow for the fact that most teachers in England and Wales do not receive the London allowance. The corrected figure is £1 692. This includes the cost of superannuation and national insurance, but can take no account of salary increases under negotiation as this book goes to press.

3. A fair proportion (perhaps 40 per cent) of nursery assistants are at present untrained except through experience on the job and are on a Class II scale, ranging in 1971 from £336 at 16, by eight increments, to £612, with a London Allowance in the Metropolitan area of £90 from age 18. However, the aim is for all nursery assistants to qualify by NNEB or equivalent training for the Class I scale, ranging from £474 at 18 by eight increments to £852, with London Allowance from age 18 of £90. My estimate of about £700 as an average salary cost assumes that the vast majority will be trained and with an average of about four years of incremental service.

4. The 4+ year-group in the child population in 1971 is estimated at 826 000 (table 43). If 75 per cent were half-time and 15 per cent full-time, this comes to about 434 000 places. It can be calculated from the data in chapter 3, that the number of *places* available in maintained nursery education in January 1969 was about 74 000. So roughly 360 000 extra places (including those in the Urban Aid Programme) would need to be provided to meet the standard set.

CHAPTER 7

New Perspectives

I hope it may be thought that the pattern of early schooling proposed in this book has much to offer to children, parents and teachers. To children it offers a gradual introduction to school, beginning for many at a much earlier age than at present, and free of many of the stresses and strains imposed by present policy. To the parent it gives a very wide variety of choice within which to find the best pattern for starting school for the individual child.

To many teachers it would offer both a challenge and an opportunity: the challenge of responsibility, very often, for working with children over an age-range which bridges the present transition between nursery and infant stages; the opportunity, looking wider, of seeing the education of young children as a continuous whole, from three to eight. It is this new perspective in particular that I want to consider in this final chapter.

THE EARLY YEARS

We shall approach this crucial period in a child's development with a fitting humility if we look back for a moment at what he has already achieved. In early infancy he has come through (in Piaget and Inhelder's happy phrase*) the 'Copernican revolution' in which he begins to draw a clear distinction between himself and other things, with himself no longer at the centre. He has gained a gradual mastery of the perplexing rules that govern the behaviour of things in his immediate environment. For example, he has come to realise that objects have a continuing permanence

* J. Piaget, and B. Inhelder, *The Psychology of the Child* (English edition, Routledge and Kegan Paul 1969).

165

when they are out of sight, and that they are constant in size and shape, despite the tricks of perspective. And he has already begun to gather 'know-how' about the simplest elements of physical causality—for example, that drawing a mat towards him will bring a desired object with it, if the object is on the mat, but not if it is on the floor beside it.

These, and others like them, are tremendous achievements, fundamental to future learning. But at least we can begin to see, however dimly, the kind of way in which they come about. The child's linguistic achievement, over the same period, is a very different matter, for here the mind boggles in even beginning to try to explain it. We may think with Chomsky, that the child may possess an innate disposition to develop his understanding of language along the broad lines of a 'universal grammar'. But this will, at best, only give him a start towards an understanding of the structure of his own language. This is not given him on a plate; he has to construct it, *ab initio*, for himself, presumably by some process of induction, by abstracting accepted usage out of the multiplicity of utterances that occur around him, few of them directed at him. From this miscellaneous bombardment, he must gradually refine his grasp of the meanings of words, both in their connotation and denotation. He must also become familiar with the relation of word-order to meaning, and the other rules of syntax. All this also, he must achieve by induction, by abstracting significant regularities and discarding accidentals. We must remember, further, that he is having to undertake this fantastic sorting operation with the material of a language he has hardly begun to understand, which he is learning from scratch, and also that he is doing it, at the age of one to three, as a side-line to the practical occupations which are his prime concern. Which of us, as adults, surrounded, shall we say, by a Swahili-speaking community, and compelled to use and hear only that language without help, would find it easy to construct for ourselves its vocabulary and syntax? Most of us would give up, with the cry, 'My kingdom for a computer!' on our lips.

Indeed, in its linguistic achievements, the child's mind, from one to three, has powers which in some respects exceed those of a computer. In some other respects it resembles a cybernetic mechanism constantly adjusting itself in the light of feed-back information from its surroundings. The mental schemata which a young child uses in his attempts to manipulate his environment are under constant revision against the test of practice. The fashioning of concepts to match the constant elements in his environment may proceed in a like manner, with constant adjustment from feed-back. The key, at first roughly-fashioned, comes by daily wear to fit the lock; and as time goes on, master keys are made and put to use, to fit a range of locks; the power to move from particular concepts to more general ones is on its way. Soon also, words provide labels which not only make communication possible, but give speed and precision to the manipulation of concepts in the mind.

CHILDREN'S THINKING IN TRANSITION

These achievements in the first three years of life are so remarkable, that one might be tempted to suppose that, by the middle of the three-to-eight period, children's thinking would be very like adults', lacking only the knowledge that comes from experience or that is conveyed, as information, from others. This is not so, as Piaget's work, spread over nearly half a century, has shown us. The very machinery of children's thinking is in constant transition. Let us take some examples.

We adults think of the world of nature as being made up of living and non-living things, of which living things have three main characteristics: they respond, they grow, and they reproduce. To the child of up to about six the distinction is less clear. He lays all the stress on response, especially movement: things which are self-moving or self-changing—clouds, rivers, motor-cars, wind, flames—all of these are thought of as alive unless young children are taught otherwise. I was sceptical of this when I first read Piaget many years ago and I tried Piaget's question on my five-year-old daughter, who produced a rather nice example. She picked up a silver spoon. 'This is alive,' she said. This puzzled me, so I asked her why. 'Because it does this', she said, and breathed on it, so that it went dull for a moment and then, on its own, as silver does, came bright again. The spoon had responded; therefore, to the five-year-old, it was alive.

Many of the things that to the young child are alive are also thought to be animated by conscious purpose. The sun rises *in order* to give us light. Clouds gather because they will be *needed* to make night. The sun follows each of us. To the child of five or six, this is an obvious fact of nature: he walks down the street and there is the sun all the time, looking out from between the houses, following him all the way. In other words, the young child seems to endow inanimate things with personality and to think even that they have a special relationship with himself. This is rather similar to the *animism* of primitive peoples: the belief that natural objects such as the sun, clouds, wind are possessed of spirits.

Young children have great difficulty in thinking which involves relationships. All their thinking tends to be in categorical rather than relational propositions. The idea, for example, that Newcastle can be north of Hull *and* south of Edinburgh seems nonsense to the seven-year-old: how can it be *both* north and south? Faced with problems involving relational thinking, the young child is apt to retreat into simpler pseudo-explanations. For example, adults explain shadows in terms of the relation between the rays of light, the object that makes the shadow, and the surface on which the shadow is cast. Instead, the young child tends to think of shadow as a sort of substance. It comes, he says, from the big shadows outside, for example, the shadows of trees and buildings which act, as it were, as reservoirs of shadow substance; or he may think that the shadow is hidden within the object, and comes out of it. Flotation is another good example. Young children are very interested in floating, but they find it very difficult to understand. For flotation depends on the relation between two densities, the density of the object and the density of the liquid; and each of these densities is itself a relation between weight and volume. No wonder the young child finds it difficult and is apt to dodge the issue. Children of seven or eight, for example, often think that an object which will not float in a basin of water, might float if you put it on the surface of a lake: there is not enough water in the basin—it is not *strong* enough. It seems as if the matter is thought of almost in terms of an effort on the part of the water, akin to the effort we ourselves make in lifting something up. Animism has taken the place of the relational thinking that is beyond the child's power.

This limited power of the young child to think relationally may help to account for Piaget's findings, now widely familiar, on the developing notion of *conservation*, for example, that a liquid or a solid conserves its volume or weight despite changes of shape. The best-known example concerns the pouring of the same volume of liquid first into a tall narrow glass and then into a short wide one. It is the same liquid—nothing has been added or taken away—nevertheless, the child tends to judge that there is more of it when in the tall narrow glass than when in the short wide one. The crude perceptual judgement that there is more of it 'because it comes up higher' cannot yet be corrected by a realisation of the inverse *relation* between width and height.

This brings me to a final point of some importance in this apparent digression on the thinking processes of young children. Piaget and the many other workers who have conducted the above experiment have usually found that a correct judgement *and a correct verbal explanation* of it could not usually be given before about seven or eight. Other workers have found,* however, that if a correct judgement was acceptable, without a verbal explanation, this could often be obtained from children of four or five. This is one example of a fact, of great importance to teachers of young children, that much of their knowledge is, as as I have called it,† a kind of 'know-how', not yet clearly expressible in words, but none-the-less valuable as a guide to action.

---

* G. E. Gruen, 'Note on Conservation: Methodological and Definitional Considerations,' 1966, reprinted in Sigel, I. E. and Hooper, F. H. (eds.) *Logical Thinking in Children*, (Holt, Rhinehart and Wilson, 1968.)

† R. Palmer, 'Experience, Information and the Mass Media,' in *Year Book of Education*, (Evans, 1960.)

Working a see-saw is an excellent example. It must surely give children, even at the nursery stage, the beginnings of 'know-how' about levers—the notion that the further you sit from the middle, the more effective is your downward push. Watch young children on a see-saw and it is clear that they possess this 'know-how'—it guides their movements. They cannot, at this stage, express this knowledge in words, generalise it in even the simple terms I have just used. But their bodies know it through experience, and that is a step towards generalised and verbalised knowledge that we must not despise. A very great deal that the nursery child learns is of this unverbalised kind; in water-play, for example, though here opportunities are often missed; in the use of bricks which may (or may not) have valuable mathematical proportions. And the constructive activities abound in opportunities to provide scientific as well as creative and imaginative experiences, for gaining 'know-how' about the properties of materials and the way they behave. Children discover, for example, about textures: rough, smooth, sticky, bumpy, and so on; that some things are light for their volume and others are heavy—what they will, much later, call a difference of density. They find that some things are elastic and others brittle and others again pliable, and that some things are harder than others. Such discoveries, and much else besides, provide the beginnings of scientific knowledge, much of it as yet unverbalised— though soon they must be helped to find the right words for it.

'To find the right words for it.' Yes indeed; for whatever may be the value of 'know-how' as a step towards knowledge, we are now in no doubt of the vital importance of language, not merely in the communication of thought, but in its organisation. It is the prime means through which one's own experience is set in order and the experience of other people added to it. So the development of an elaborated code of language is an essential basis for future learning, both about the material environment and about one's relations with other people. And it is, of course, more than this: a delight in itself, and a means to imaginative expression.

A HIGH TASK

By this point, if not before, the reader, carried along I hope by the intrinsic interest of the subject, may yet have begun to wonder where all this was leading. The answer is two-fold. In the first place, even so brief and elementary a discussion of children's thinking brings home to one afresh that working with and talking with young children is a highly-skilled job, demanding at its best a degree of sophisticated understanding which we are only just beginning to appreciate. The environment that is created for young children's learning, the explorations they make in it, the equipment that is offered them, the use they make of that, the questions they ask, and the answers they get: all of these have their impacts on the complex development of concepts and understandings and language skills. Nursery teachers can hold their heads high that they are engaged in so skilled a task, no whit less demanding intellectually than work in other stages of education. Incidentally, as I indicated on page 104, one might think this complex educational process to be beyond the intellectual competence of any but the most exceptional nursery assistant, however devoted, even with occasional supervision.

Indeed, (and this is my second point) when one considers the magnitude of the task, one begins to wonder whether the qualified nursery teacher has hitherto been sufficiently equipped to deal with the subtleties of intellectual development at this crucial stage. In many ways her training was excellent and on the social aspects of child development she will have learnt much that is of practical use. In its cognitive aspects, she will have heard something of the theory—and may then have become sadly aware of an unfilled gap between theory and practice. Despite a vast corpus of Piagetian and other research on child development, far too little has as yet been done to discover with precision its applications in the day-to-day work of the nursery and infant teacher. It is not just that we don't know *all* the answers, but that, in detail, we know hardly any. This may seem a gloomy conclusion; in fact, it is one of hope. The nursery-infant* teacher of the future, if she rises to the intellectual demands of her high task, may find herself the agent of a real revolution in learning, with its impact on all the later stages. As Plowden (para. 550) so well puts it:

'What is immediately needed is that teachers should bring to bear on their day-to-day problems astringent intellectual scrutiny. Yet all good teachers must work intuitively and be sensitive to the emotive and imaginative needs of their children. Teaching is an art and, as long as that with all its implications is firmly grasped, it will not be harmed by intellectual stiffening.'

WORKING TOGETHER

Meanwhile, the nursery and infant teachers of the present will need to get together (as some have already) to discover how best they can create a genuine continuity between the two stages, with the limited knowledge we have. In so doing, there may need to be some shift in attitudes, which have not always been in complete accord, though increasingly they are so.

Nursery teachers have been the pioneers in recognising the value of freely-chosen activities, using the resources of a richly-varied environment, in the classroom and beyond. As Plowden says (para. 523):

'. . . play is the principal means of learning in early childhood. It is the way through which children reconcile their inner lives with external reality. In play, children gradually develop concepts of causal relationships, the power to discriminate, to make judgements, to analyse and synthesise, to imagine and to formulate.'

Infant teachers have learnt from the nursery school the value of free play, and themselves have discovered the many ways in which, at the infant stage, it can give point and purpose to the

* If, in future, the roles are less distinct, we may need at least to hyphenate the titles!

basic skills. Nevertheless, some difference in emphasis between nursery and infant teachers is sometimes discernable. Infant teachers, preoccupied not unnaturally with 'getting them on', may sometimes underestimate the importance of play and the vital contribution it can make to children's progress, not least in the three Rs. Conversely, nursery teachers (and especially, perhaps, those working in nursery classes under infant or primary heads) may be concerned lest the particular value of free play to children of three and four should be lost through some premature attempt to introduce at that age the first steps in the basic skills. How can these points of view be reconciled?

Let me say at once that the best ultimate hope for complete reconciliation lies, as I see it, in an overlapping continuity of the two stages, such as the *London Plan* would provide, so that nursery-infant teachers would see themselves as concerned with the *same* task, the education of young children. Between them, and with the help of other experts, they might then gradually discover the ways in which the theoretical knowledge we now have could be applied in practice to the needs of children of different ages. But that is a task for the future. Meanwhile we can begin to see smaller adjustments that could be made.

In the first place, it may well be that some nursery teachers should more often be willing to consider the needs of the exceptional child. It can happen, for example, that a bright child of four may enter a nursery school or class already—without pressure—having acquired a grounding in reading and writing at home. Sometimes, because the nursery teacher feels that reading and writing are 'for infants', the child gets little encouragement to use his skills at school. This seems a pity when the rich environment of a good nursery class could offer much scope for their use. In general, we are beginning to realise that the concept of 'readiness', whether for reading or anything else, is suspect if linked too rigidly to particular ages or stages. In the education of young children, the first guiding principle must be that 'children vary'.

Secondly, and on a much wider front, we need to consider whether some of the play material of the nursery stage can be selected or adapted or designed in such a way that it provides insights or removes barriers of specific importance in later learning. What could turn out to be an excellent example derives from some research done by Dr Elizabeth Newson some years ago.* She investigated the capacity of children of four and five to discriminate between shapes which are mirror-images—differing in the same sort of way as d and b or p and q differ—though in fact she did not use letters, but shapes that were specially devised. She found that many of these young children were unable to make these discriminations; it appeared that they simply could not perceive the differences. However, some of them could; and she found further that these children, who at just five were good at this kind of discrimination, when they were followed through the infant school became, as a rule, good readers.

In fact, it turned out that their performance in this test at five provided a better predictor of their reading and writing skills at $6\frac{1}{2}$ than did their intelligence. This suggests very strongly that the incapacity to discriminate mirror-image shapes may, for many children, be a strong hindrance in the early stages of reading, so that children who already possess this capacity at five get off to a flying start. Meanwhile, Dr Newson had been trying out play material designed to give practice in this kind of discrimination— for example, specially made form-boards, wire shapes, etc. And she found that four-year-olds, after only twenty minutes of practice with this material, under supervision, raised their score on her test above that of five-year-old children. In short, if there is a discrimination-lack in young children which acts as a hindrance to the acquisition of reading skill, it looks as if this barrier could quite easily be removed. It ought to be said that some further tentative experiments† in which infant teachers made this practice material available as part of the play equipment of five-year-olds, were inconclusive. However, there is clearly something here which merits further study.

An incidental point arising out of this example is just worth

---

* E. Newson, *The Development of Line Figure Discrimination in Pre-school Children* (Ph.D. Thesis, University of Nottingham, 1956).

† E. Newson, *Learning to Write: an Investigation* (University of Nottingham Institute of Education Bulletin, 29, 1958).

mention. For some years, progressive nursery and infant teachers have tended to look down their noses at form-boards and jig-saws because, too often in the past, they tended to be used merely as 'occupations' for young children, who it was thought would be better involved in more creative and exploratory activities. Their instinct was right but, if form-boards and jig-saws, *suitably designed*, have an important contribution to make to perceptual skills, then in practice they were wrong. How true it is that 'we don't know all the answers'!

And the main point of this example follows on from what I have just said. We simply do not know how the design of nursery play-material can influence the acquisition of skills at the infant stage. This is a matter of research and the research has not been done. The example given could be one such field of study: the inclusion among the play-material available at the nursery stage of a great profusion of interesting equipment, specially designed, while giving young children pleasure, to help them surmount this discriminatory barrier. The same kind of situation almost certainly occurs in the field of mathematical experience. We know a good deal now about the early growth of mathematical concepts, but very little with any certainty about how such theoretical knowledge can be applied in the design of bricks for use at the nursery stage, not to mention the many other kinds of mathematical experience through play that could be made available.

Nursery teachers are rightly concerned that the key position of play at the nursery stage should remain inviolate. This is not in question. What is here suggested is something quite different from the premature introduction of direct teaching of the three Rs to children who are far from ready for it. All that is proposed is that in the design and selection of nursery play material we should sometimes take cognisance of its effect, where this can be established, on the acquisition of skills at a later stage.

This brings me to a final suggestion for collaboration, now, between nursery and infant teachers. I have emphasised more than once how little we know, in practical terms, of the later effects of equipment and procedures at the nursery stage. A great body of action research is urgently needed. And it so happens that we have already in existence a magnificent control situation for carrying it out. Nearly 40 000 children are in half-time nursery education. How easy it would be to take say, a dozen nursery classes, twenty-four groups of children, some morning, some afternoon. To a dozen groups, six morning and six afternoon, one would make available a piece of equipment or a procedure to be tested. The other twelve would act as controls. All the children would then go on (as they now do) to the same twelve infant or primary schools, with the experimentals and controls mixed in classes under the same teachers. And there, in due time, any effect of the equipment or procedure could be tested. This beautifully controlled situation, which might have been specially designed to gladden the heart of a research worker, has existed for years, and we have done nothing to make use of it. At a time when there is some concern about progress in reading, a large-scale study of the effect on this of various kinds of nursery equipment and procedure would seem to have considerable priority, but one hopes too that the mathematicians would not be slow in coming forward with ideas to be tested. But such studies need not be limited to the investigation of the effect of nursery equipment and procedures on later learning of the basic skills. It is possible also that ways of working that affect the social relationships and groupings and attitudes of children at the nursery stage might also prove to have long-term consequences which it would be of value to know about.

I leave the reader with this exciting prospect of a future in which nursery and infant teachers sink their separate identities in working together to bring our new knowledge of early childhood to bear on the education of young children which is their common concern.

Appendix

The London Plan: Studies in Peckham and Brixton

Documentation to satisfy the experts can be a dreary business, and I cannot commend this appendix to the more general reader as affording much delight or inspiration. Nevertheless, the claims of the *London Plan* to be an *easily workable* pattern for starting school rest very considerably on the detailed studies which were made of the way it would work if applied to the actual circumstances, in 1969, of forty London schools. If these claims, and the evidence on which they are based, are to be taken seriously, then the nature of that evidence needs to be sufficiently explained and put on record, so that its validity can be judged. That is the purpose of this appendix.

GENERAL

Some account has already been given in chapter 6 of these studies in Peckham and Brixton. As there explained, the general principle of the investigation was to gather for each school information on the number and size of rooms in use for infants (and for the nursery class, if any), to estimate the current annual intake, and then to fit the children to the rooms available, in accordance with the principles of the plan. When the age-groups whose attendance, half-time or full-time, is compulsory under the plan had been provided for, it was then possible to see in what numbers the rest of the 4+ year-group and some of the 3+ year-group could be accommodated on a voluntary basis, usually half-time but sometimes full-time. When this had been done for all twenty schools in an area, the total numbers in each term-age-group who could be placed in school in each of the three terms could be found, and expressed as a percentage of the total term-age-group. On the basis of this information, one could then calculate the distribution of ages of entry to school, for each term-age-group, and also the average age of entry to school. Similar information could also be calculated for entry to full-time attendance. In addition, it was possible by a further detailed scrutiny of the sheets for individual schools, to gather a good deal of other information about the way the plan would work out. Such use of the data is illustrated on pages 137-9 and 141.

In what follows, further information will be given about the steps in this process, the standards applied, and the results obtained.

THE AREAS STUDIED

A very brief account has already been given (pages 144-5) of the characteristics of the Peckham and Brixton areas. Here it is only necessary to state how the areas were defined. The 'Peckham area' did not cover the whole of the Peckham parliamentary division, but included the twenty schools comprised in the Catchment Areas III-VIII, two of the schools being actually in Deptford. The 'Brixton area' was defined so as to include twenty schools within a radius of about three-quarters of a mile of Lambeth Town Hall. A nursery school, exactly on the edge of the Brixton area, was excluded from consideration since its contribution to most of the schools concerned was likely to be small.

ANNUAL INTAKE

With six exceptions, the annual intake was taken as the average of the 5+ and 6+ year-groups in the school in January 1969. The annual intake of a school may vary a little from year to year, often on account of temporary housing situations, and it was thought safer to average two recent year-groups rather than to rely on the most recent, i.e. the 5+ year-group. In two schools in Peckham, however, it was clear from an analysis of the age-composition of the school or from other information that numbers were about to rise rapidly, and an adjustment was made to allow for this. In one other school in Peckham and three in Brixton, numbers were being built up to fill new or extended accommodation, so that the 1969 numbers were gross underestimates of the normal future intake. In these cases the annual intake assumed for calculation was that which would fill the number of classes the school was intended to have eventually.

These schools have been opened or extended in order to relieve pressure on neighbouring schools but, in dealing with these neighbouring schools, no allowance for such relief has been made, it being assumed, pessimistically, that the new or extended schools will do little more than avoid there being a surplus of children. My assumptions, therefore, in these few uncertain cases, were on the safe side.

In reckoning the numbers of 3+ and 4+ children available to enter schools in Peckham without a nursery class, a small correction had to be made in order to allow for the effect of the local nursery school. This contributes to the size of the 5+ year-group in local primary schools, but would continue to cater for these children at 3+ and 4+, so a small deduction, proportionate to roll, had to be made from the annual intake of schools without a nursery class, to allow for this. At present the annual output of the nursery school is about 48 children a year, all of whom have attended part-time. It was assumed that, under the *London Plan*, the annual output would be reduced to about 36 children, 12 of whom would have attended full-time from 3+. If it was thought necessary to increase the 3+ full-time percentage (see page 147), this nursery could become full-time only.

ACCOMMODATION

Plans of each school were studied and every room listed with particulars of its floor area. Only those rooms now used as infant or nursery classrooms (or, in schools building up, intended for such use) were reckoned as available for class purposes under the *London Plan*. In other words, rooms now used as amenity rooms would be retained as such. Clearly, if they were used to ease the implementation of the plan, this would be at some cost to the standards available to the older infants, which would be unacceptable. In allocating rooms between the older children on infant standards and the younger children on nursery standards, it was obviously advantageous logistically if the younger children could have fair-sized rooms; for example, a room of only 400 sq.ft would allow, on nursery standards, for a class of only 16, which would be costly in staff. However, a good deal of care was taken—under the eagle eye of my infants' colleague—to play fair by the children of present infant age, and to ensure that they had a reasonable proportion of the good-sized rooms. Otherwise their activities would be limited and the standard of infant work diminished in order to ease the implementation of the plan—which again would be unacceptable. In allocating rooms to the younger children, some attention was paid to their possibilities for sanitary adaptations—though obviously this could not be done with much precision without on-the-spot study by architects.

Only in one case was a room at present belonging to the junior department assumed to be taken over for infant use. This was in a case where a junior department of 235 in seven classes had the use of thirteen rooms, and it was felt that a slightly fairer allocation of accommodation between departments was in any case overdue.

Six schools, two in Peckham and four in Brixton, were about to acquire a nursery class under the first phase of the Urban Aid Programme. These nursery classrooms were to be sufficiently spacious to provide for forty children in the morning and forty in the afternoon, with two nursery assistants instead of one to assist the qualified teacher. The existence of these rooms (now in operation) and of the staff authorised for them was assumed when the cases of these schools were dealt with.

STANDARDS

Different standards of roll and accommodation were adopted (as at present) for children of present infant age—rising-five and upwards, and for children of present nursery age—less than rising-five. Where a class contained *only* children of present infant age, in a given term, its maximum permitted roll, for the purposes of the exercise, was taken as the average infant class roll in that school in summer 1969. The highest rolls found, both in Peckham and Brixton, were forties, and the medians 37 in Peckham and 38 in Brixton.* It seemed fair to take the summer roll, even though this was usually the highest in the year, since in the *London Plan* exercise also, classes could often be kept well below this figure in the other two terms.

When a class contained, in a given term, *any* children of under rising-five, it was held to a roll which would allow 25 sq.ft per pupil; e.g. in a room of 500 sq.ft, this would mean not more than 20 pupils, or in a room of 750 sq.ft, not more than 30. But even if the room exceeded 750 sq.ft, the roll was held to the normal nursery-class maximum of 30. The only exceptions were the six rooms designed under the Urban Aid Programme to provide for forty children at a time.

Since, under the plan, some classes tend, in some terms, to contain a mixture of rising-fives with some children who are a little younger, this means that the rising-fives would often benefit from nursery standards of accommodation and roll, required because of the inclusion in the class of younger children. The nursery standard of accommodation did not, however, necessarily apply to a class throughout the year; if, perhaps in the summer term, *all* the children in a class had reached rising-five or over, then the roll could be allowed to rise to that of the present

* Almost inevitably, it will be claimed that, in order to make the plan work, I have assumed infant class rolls rising in some cases to forties. Fair-minded critics, however, will realise that these exercises necessarily took the Peckham and Brixton situation *as it actually existed in 1969*, to provide a firm base-line for testing the feasibility of the *London Plan* under known conditions at a given point in time. If, as the ILEA is now endeavouring to do, maximum infant class rolls are limited to 35, this can only be achieved, in many cases, by providing extra rooms and teachers. If the plan would work in 1969, with maximum infant class rolls of 40, it would then also work, with these additional resources, and a maximum infant class roll of 35. Furthermore, the plan does provide, incidentally, some marginal improvement in standards for the younger infants, even under 1969 conditions.

average infant class in the school. On the other hand, as we have seen (pages 140–1), if a class justified a nursery assistant early in the year when some of the children were of present nursery age, her services would be retained throughout the year, even though, in a later term, all might be of present infant age.

All the data given in the text on the operation of the *London Plan* in these forty schools are based on an analysis which employed the above strict nursery standard for children of present nursery age. However, when the Peckham study was planned, it was thought worth while to conduct it three times over, using in each operation a different standard for these younger children. The three standards were:

1. *Nursery Standard*: as above, viz. 25 sq.ft per pupil; maximum class roll 30.
2. *Compromise Standard*: 17·5 sq.ft per pupil; maximum class roll 35.
3. *Infant Standard*. At least 10 sq.ft per pupil; maximum class roll—the summer 1969 average for an infant class in the school.

No one really believed that an infant standard ought to be applied if the class contained any children of nursery age; even so, it was thought worth while to see what effect the use of this standard, for the younger children as well as the older ones, would have on the logistics of the plan. It can be said at once that the gains, though substantial, were not spectacular. Thus in Peckham the average percentage of 3+ children who could attend half-time was raised from 38 per cent on nursery standard to 53 per cent on infant standard, and the average age of entry to school lowered by about two months. These logistic gains did not seem in any way to justify the lowering of standards of nursery accommodation and roll that would be entailed. An investigation of the results of applying an infant standard to the younger children was therefore omitted from the Brixton study. An analysis using the compromise standard was, however, retained in both the Peckham and the Brixton studies, for comparison with the results obtained using the nursery standard. After all, some nursery classes are doing good work in rooms which approximate to the Compromise Standard, and it was thought that the use of this standard here and there as a temporary measure might help to solve some logistic problems. In fact, it did not. For example, the two schools in Peckham in which the compulsory requirements of the plan could not be wholly met without an additional classroom, still required this addition even when a Compromise Standard was used for the younger children. And the over-all effect on the Plowden percentages was not great.

It is, perhaps, a moot point whether it was worth while to repeat this gruelling operation a total of a hundred times for the forty schools, in order to establish this somewhat negative conclusion. Certainly, at the end of the road, I was glad to be relieved of any necessity to consider further the acceptance, under the *London Plan*, of conditions which fell short of the highest nursery standards—even if only 'as a temporary measure' in particular cases of difficulty.

METHOD OF ANALYSIS

When the roll and accommodation data for a school had been collected and studied, the next step was to choose and set aside a sufficient number of rooms for the children of 5+ and 6+, using as a divisor the average infant class roll in summer 1969. When this had been done, there might be a few children of 5+ left over, who would need to be found places, full-time, in one of the younger classes; sometimes, however, there might be room in a 5+ class for a few children of 4+. After making these adjustments, one was left, usually, with a full 4+ year-group, and as many as possible of the 3+ year-group, to be accommodated, according to the principles of the plan, in the rooms remaining.

The next step was to split the 4+ year-group into its three term-age-groups (TAG), since these required separate treatment. This was done on the rough-and-ready basis of dividing the total number of the year-group by three, rather than by calculating the numbers on the 33:28:39 ratio arrived at on page 116. It is unlikely that this approximation will have affected the results appreciably, especially as the autumn-born, which most often gave some logistic trouble, are in any case almost precisely one-third of a year-group.

When this had been done (making allowance, where necessary, for a few 4+ children, usually autumn-born, who might have been placed in older classes), one could then get on with planning the age-composition of each of the younger classes. It was essential to begin this process with the summer term and work backwards through the year, since children who could not be accommodated in the summer term must not be found a place earlier. In filling up the rooms, it was first necessary to ensure that places were found for children required by the plan to attend either full-time or half-time, in a given term; when this had been done, first priority tended to be given to half-time voluntary attendance at 4+, and the places that were left could then be allocated to children of 3+, half-time. However, in some schools where there was ample room, some full-time places were set aside for the voluntary attendance of children, usually of 4+ but sometimes of 3+ also. In general, however, the requirements which governed the allocation were as follows (TAG = term-age-group; N denotes that the children in question must be on nursery standards in that term):

SUMMER TERM
Full-time: (i) Any 5+ children over from other rooms.
        (ii) Autumn-born 4+ (compulsory) = TAG.
Half-time: (i) Spring and summer-born 4+ = 2 TAG.
        (ii) 3+ children for whom there is room. (N)

SPRING TERM
Full-time: (i) Any 5+ children over from other rooms.
Half-time: (i) Autumn-born 4+ (compulsory) = TAG.
        (ii) Spring-born 4+ (voluntary but say 100%) = TAG.
        (iii) Summer-born 4+ (voluntary but say 100%) = TAG (N)
        (iv) 3+ children for whom there is room, but not in excess of summer numbers. (N)

AUTUMN TERM

Full-time: (i) Any 5+ children over from other rooms.

Half-time: (i) Autumn-born 4+ (voluntary but say 100%) = TAG.

    (ii) Spring-born 4+ (voluntary but say 100%) = TAG. (N)

    (iii) Summer-born 4+ (voluntary but say 100%) = TAG. (N)

    (iv) 3+ children for whom there is room, but not in excess of spring numbers. (N)

By applying these principles to any particular room, it was possible to arrive at a formula for each room, for each term, which described, separately for morning and afternoon sessions, the precise composition of the class in terms of the numbers of children of each age-group. In arriving at this formula, account was taken of:

1. Whether the class as a whole was on nursery or on infant standards—if *any* were below rising-five it was on nursery standards.
2. The size of the room.
3. In relation to this, the maximum roll allowed on infant or on nursery standards, as the case might be.

When all this had been done for a particular school—the class compositions being worked out on a duplicated sheet—it was usually found that all the 4+ children could be accommodated from the beginning of the school year, and it was assumed that they would so attend. In other words, if attendance was voluntary, it was assumed that the places would be taken up, where available, 100 per cent, and that where it was compulsory, no 'opting out' would be sought. In so far as these assumptions were incorrect, the actual logistics would be that much more favourable for the admission of younger children and for full-time provision.

It will be seen above that we also arrived at a figure for the number of 3+ children who could be accommodated half-time, term by term. It was now necessary to make an arbitrary decision as to how this number was likely to be divided among the term-age-groups, since attendance was voluntary. In doing this, it was assumed that autumn-born children would most often seek to attend, or would be given preference, because they were older. On the other hand, this bias was exercised in moderation, the aim being to ensure that the summer-born gained half-time admission a little younger than did the spring and summer-born, so as to provide some compensation for the handicap of being young within the year-group. Let me give a fairly typical example. The number of children of 3+ who could be accommodated half-time in the autumn term was 34, rising to 42 in the spring and summer terms. This was out of a total year-group of 99. Arbitrarily, these total numbers were assumed to be distributed as follows:

	Autumn term	*Spring term*	*Summer term*
Autumn-born	16	18	18
Spring-born	10	14	14
Summer-born	8	10	10
	34	42	42

The average age of entry to half-time schooling was then calculated for this distribution and came out at: autumn-born—4:3⅔, spring-born—4:1⅓, summer-born—3:10⅔. In short, my trial guess at the appropriate numbers within the termly totals had been a good one, and as a result the summer-born had been allowed some compensatory advantage, in having, on average, a slightly earlier age of entry.

This calculation completed the analysis for each school. It was now necessary to pool the results for all twenty schools in an area. This was done by tabulating for all the schools the number of children of 3+ and 4+, by term-age-groups, who could be placed in school half-time or full-time, in each term of the year. A separate, but similar table showed the numbers of children who could be given full-time schooling earlier than was compulsory under the plan. The numbers were added up and the totals expressed as percentages of the total term-age-group in the area. Then, by counting backwards from the age at which attendance was 100 per cent, one could arrive at the percentages entering school half-time or full-time at various ages.

Strictly speaking, these data referred to entry over an age-range of four months. For example, in Peckham it was found that 37 per cent of the autumn-born could enter school between 3:8 and 4:0, the variation being due to their birthdays scattering throughout the autumn term. For simplicity in calculation, this was shown as entry at the mid-point of the range, i.e. 3:10, and similarly in other cases.

Finally, from these percentage distributions, it was possible to calculate the average age of entry, to school and to full-time, for a given term-age-group, and the over-all averages for the year-group. In the year-group averages, weighting for the varying sizes of the three term-age-groups was done.

RESULTS OF THE EXERCISES

Peckham

The over-all percentages attending half-time and full-time at 3+ and 4+ have been tabulated on page 146 with the Plowden percentages in brackets for comparison. In more detail, the percentage of 3+ children in school, whether half-time or full-time, ranged from 30 per cent (summer-born in autumn-term) to 52 per cent (autumn-born in summer term). The percentage of 4+ children in school ranged from 89 per cent (summer-born in autumn-term) up to 100 per cent in most other cases. The age of entry to school distributed in detail as follows:

	Autumn-born			*Spring-born*			*Summer-born*	
5% at 3:2			5% at 3:2			30% at 3:2		
37% at 3:10	Aver-		31% at 3:6	Aver-		5% at 3:6	Aver-	
6% at 4:2	age		3% at 3:10	age		1% at 3:10	age	
4% at 4:6	4:4		1% at 4:2	4:1		53% at 4:2	3:10½	
48% at 4:10			59% at 4:6			5% at 4:6		
			1% at 4:10			6% at 4:10		

The weighted over-all average is 4:1.

The percentages of 4+ children able to attend voluntarily full-time ranged from 5 per cent (summer-born children in autumn and spring) to 41 per cent (autumn-born children in the spring term). In addition, 4 per cent of the autumn-born 3+ children and 2 per cent of the spring-born 3+ children could attend full-time, throughout the year. The detailed distribution for age of entry to full-time schooling was as follows:

	Autumn-born			*Spring-born*			*Summer-born*	
4% at 3:10	Aver-		2% at 3:6			5% at 4:2	Aver-	
33% at 4:10	age		4% at 4:6	Aver-		1% at 4:10	age	
4% at 5:2	5:2½		5% at 4:10	age		94% at 5:2	5:1⅓	
59% at 5:6			4% at 5:2	5:4½				
			85% at 5:6					

The weighted over-all average is 5:2⅔.

Brixton

Here again, the over-all percentages have been tabulated on page 150. In more detail, the percentages of 3+ children in school, whether half-time or full-time, ranged from 24 per cent (summer-born in autumn term) to 48 per cent (autumn-born in summer term). The percentage of 4+ children in school ranged from 98 per cent (summer-born in autumn) to 100 per cent (all other cases). The age of entry to school distributed in detail as follows:

Autumn-born		*Spring-born*		*Summer-born*	
44% at 3:10	Aver-age 4:4¾	33% at 3:6	Aver-age 4:1½	24% at 3:2	Aver-age 3:10¾
3% at 4:2		5% at 3:10		5% at 3:6	
1% at 4:6		2% at 4:2		2% at 3:10	
52% at 4:10		60% at 4:6		67% at 4:2	
				2% at 4:10	

The weighted over-all average is 4:1½.

No children of 3+ could be accepted full-time, and the percentages of 4+ children who could attend voluntarily full-time ranged from 0 per cent (summer-born children in autumn and spring) to 20 per cent (autumn-born children in spring). The detailed distribution for age of entry to full-time schooling was as follows:

Autumn-born		*Spring-born*		*Summer-born*	
18% at 4:10	Aver-age 5:4½	5% at 4:6	Aver-age 5:5	13% at 4:10	Aver-age 5:1½
2% at 5:2		10% at 5:2		87% at 5:2	
80% at 5:6		85% at 5:6			

The weighted over-all average is 5:3½.

EFFECT OF PHASED IMPLEMENTATION

The above results assume, as discussed on pages 146 and 150, that in two schools in Peckham and eight in Brixton an additional classroom would be made available, since otherwise the compulsory requirements of the plan could not be fully realised in these schools, in the sense that some summer-born children would not be able to attend half-time in the summer term before their full-time entry. It was suggested that, in some authorities, this compulsory requirement might be waived, at least until a date to be arranged, or until it was found whether voluntary attendance for these children would meet the situation satisfactorily. Such phased implementation would obviate the need, in most of these cases, for additional rooms or teachers.

Thus, in Peckham, the two additional classrooms would not be needed, nor would it be necessary to transfer a room in one school from junior use. There would be no increase at all in teaching staff over present numbers. The effect on age of entry to school was quite negligible: an over-all average of 4:2 instead of 4:1. On average, 36 per cent of the 3+ children (as against 40 per cent) and 95 per cent of the 4+ children (as against 98 per cent) would be in school.

In Brixton, the savings and losses would both be more marked. Seven of the eight additional classrooms would not be required and the increase in teaching staff would be reduced from 5·7 per cent to 0·5 per cent. But the over-all average age of entry to school would be raised from 4:1½ to 4:4½. On average only 20 per cent of the 3+ children (as against 37 per cent) and 90 per cent of the 4+ children (as against 100 per cent) would be in school.

As we have seen, Brixton is a neighbourhood of extreme difficulty, and it seems likely that the quite moderate effects of phased implementation in Peckham may be more characteristic of the country as a whole. On the other hand, the gains also, judged by the Peckham experience, might be quite small.

Index